| | |
|---|---|
| Editorials | 2 |
| Reviews | 3 |
| Interview with Yaphet Kotto | 17 |
| Cryptid Files: The Killer Shews | 21 |
| Director Spotlight: Vinod Talwar | 24 |
| Astron-6 Adam Brooks interview | 29 |
| Las Vegas Bloodbath | 33 |
| Growing Up Exploited | 36 |
| The Take-Away, Pt. 2 | 38 |
| THE BOOKSHELF | 50 |

Cover art: David Barnes

September 2012

**Brian Harris, Editor & Publisher**
**Timothy Paxton, Editor & Design**

WENG'S CHOP is published quarterly. © 2012 Wildside Publishing / Kronos Productions. All rights reserved. No part of this publication may be reproduced, distributed, or transmitted in any form or by any means, including photocopying, recording, or other electronic or mechanical methods, without the prior written permission of the publisher, except in the case of brief quotations embodied in critical reviews and certain other noncommercial uses permitted by copyright law. For permission requests, write to the publisher, addressed "Attention: Permissions Coordinator," at the address below. 4301 Sioux Lane #1, McHenry, IL 60050, United States
w i l d s i d e c i n e m a @ c o m c a s t . n e t
Volume #1 / Issue #1 / 2nd Printing

# A WORD FROM THE EDITORS...

## Brian's Smutatorial

So after reading the last issue (#0) cover to cover I figured some readers may experience some confusion when it comes to some of the films reviewed. I mean, how in hell would one actually find those films? Where would you even start looking? Do they seek out the VHS, LD, VCD, DVD or BD? How much should they expect to pay? Well, the answer is simple, by any means necessary in any format you can get your hands on, the cheaper the better. The object of our reviews is to get folks to check the films out but as cult cinema fans often discover, not every film will be readily available for rental or stateside purchase, some films may be OOP (and expensive), some may be floating about on auction sites (and insanely expensive) and others may only be available overseas. Here's the thing, entertainment value is king, not monetary value. These reviews and articles aren't a guide to collecting rarity for the chest-beaters but a helping hand to experiencing hard-to-find entertainment. If that means paying a few bucks for some VCDs, do it! If that means locating a 3rd generation Malaysian VHS rip, do it! Check your local Redbox, Walmart bins and Netflix as well, you'd be surprised what you might find. What is truly entertaining cinema worth to you? Well, only you can answer that question, but hopefully WENG'S CHOP can point you in the right direction. If not, beat a midgets ass for that shit... or is that beat a leprechaun's ass? Hmm...

## Tim's Back History

The first draft of my editorial was a cut and dry account of how I survived the 20 year assault of the Z-Wars; the struggle, blood, sweat, sex, but no tears (I rarely cry for some reason). The result was a mound of zines including six of my own. But I won't bother to dredge up ancient history as I left the scene in 1996 intending never to return.

Then in 2011 Brian contacted me via Facebook. He wanted to know if I would be interested in being interviewed for his radio show "Pieces with Brian Harris". I am constantly surprised to hear that any one of my publications may have been an important zine in some way or another. My sales were abysmal and subscription base was very small. However, after two fun interviews Brian told me about the Print-On-Demand scene. And did I ant to work with him designing a new fanzine? I got sucked back in.

Thank you, Brian!!!

I hadn't written for so many years I was afraid that I couldn't come up with anything original to say.

You know, the Internet and all.

But, that doesn't matter because you're reading this you have Weng's Chop #1 in your hands RIGHT NOW! "My hands? What are you psychic?" HUH? Yes, holding this material object means you have a paper-based zine, something that you can lug around with you and read whenever you like. You have no need to plug anything in, other than maybe a lamp to illuminate this manuscript.

Love me some paper products.

So there you go. Oh, for those of you who want to explore The Wonderful World of Zine, Books, Periodicals, and other Realworld (as opposed to cloud based) Literature turn to page 50 NOW.

See you in three months or thereabouts.

# ...ABOUT THE CONTRIBUTORS

**Bennie Woodell** is a filmmaker born and raised in Chicago, now living the dream in LA. Hong Kong cinema is his passion, looking up to Wong Kar-Wai, Chang Cheh, and Johnnie To as his main inspirations. Woodell has directed four feature films. His latest film, THE SAD CAFE, an homage to Hong Kong cinema, recently won Best Drama Feature at the Action On Film Festival in Pasadena, California. His second feature film, FAST ZOMBIES WITH GUNS, was recently released nationwide in Family Video stores by Chemical Burn Entertainment, who also distributed his third feature, DEATH ANGEL DECEMBER: VENGEANCE KILL. Woodell's favorite film is ASHES OF TIME, and thinks the best acting duo is Tony Leung Chiu-Wai and Maggie Cheung. For more information on Woodell and his films, please visit jianghuproductions.net

**Dan Taylor** has been writing about junk culture and fringe media since his zine Exploitation Retrospect debuted in 1986. 26 years later the publication is still going strong as a website, blog and -- yes -- a resurrected print edition. Check it all out at Dantenet. com, EROnline.blogspot.com or Facebook.com/ExploitationRetrospect.

**Mike Haushalter** is a lifelong film fan. He formed an anime club, Moonlight Ramblers, in 1991, and he remains president for life. When that group disbanded in 1997, he and pal Matt Gilligan started up a review and interview 'zine called Secret Scroll Digest that ran until 2005. He has worked as firearms wrangler and craft services on several Happy Cloud Pictures productions, giving him insight into life behind the camera that many film reviewers lack. His greatest film disappointment is the time his grandma promised to take him to STAR WARS, but they saw CLOSE ENCOUNTERS OF THE THIRD KIND instead.

**Phillip Escott** is a British movie lover with a boner for not just the finest trash, but the best art house. Basically he likes anything that shows boobies. When he's not admiring naked bodies he's attempting to make films. He urges/will blow you if you come and watch his 'films'. You can reach Phill through www.facebook.com/441films

**Tim Paxton** has a life-long love affair with The She Creature and harbors no shame about it. Born in Ohio to a houseful of hippies with a mom who loved horror films and comics. He was doomed from the day he entered this world.

**Brian Harris**: - can be found skipping the halls of Arborea, pondering the existence of David Lynch and plotting his next foray into the literary world. When he's not dressing up in a cowboy outfit and taping a cut-out of Franco Nero's face to his own, he's furiously masturbating to the sounds of Futurecop. Known for inspiring others, in an almost cult-like manner, Brian marches to the beat of his own drum and prefers the taste of Cherry kool-aid...so will you. You can find four of his books online, if you look hard enough, and he runs a box set blog for his own sadistic amusement.

**David Barnes** has his own line of comics and also creates vintage "grindhouse" t-shirts. His work can be seen at zid3ya@yahoo.com and myspace.com@paramere.

**Douglas Waltz** lives in the wilds of Kalamazoo, MI where he is experimenting with primitive pottery techniques. His zine, Divine Exploitation, has existed in print or online form since 1988 and can be found at http://divineexploitation.blogspot.com. His recent book, A Democrazy of Braindrained Loons; The Films of Michael Legge can be purchased at https://tsw.createspace.com/title/3814218. Douglas would like you to know that all Jess Franco films are good. ALL OF THEM!

**Stephen R. Bissette**, a pioneer graduate of the Joe Kubert School, currently teaches at the Center for Cartoon Studies and is renowned for Swamp Thing, Taboo (launching From Hell and Lost Girls), '1963,' Tyrant, co-creating John Constantine, and creating the world's second '24-Hour Comic' (invented by Scott McCloud for Bissette). He writes, illustrates, and has co-authored many books; his latest include Teen Angels & New Mutants (2011), the short story "Copper" in The New Dead (2010), and he illustrated The Vermont Monster Guide (2009). Bissette is currently completing S.R. Bissette's How to Make a Monster (Watson-Guptill/Random House) for 2014 publication.

"I was transformed at a tender age by all things monstrous: BEAST FROM 20,000 FATHOMS, THEM!, THIEF OF BAGDAD (1940), RODAN on endless play on the local afternoon TV movie; Fin Fang Foom, Tim Boo Ba, Gorgo, Konga, Reptilicus, Reptisaurus, and KONA, MONARCH OF MONSTER ISLE in comics; Charles Knight, Rudolph Zallinger, Zdenak Burian, and OLEY THE SEA MONSTER in the my town library; FAMOUS MONSTERS OF FILMLAND, CASTLE OF FRANKENSTEIN, MODERN MONSTER, and UFO zines at the newsstand; Aurora monster, Rat Fink, and Weird-Os model kits; and the giant drive-in movie ads in the weekend newspaper. Mitch Casey drew the first monster comic I ever saw crafted by human hands—"Attack of the Giant Tse-Tse Flies"—when I was six years old, and I never looked back, always ahead, making my own monster marks thereafter."

**Gary Baxter** - see page 36!

**Danae Dunning** - Goth/metal/hippie chick from Hobbs, New Mexico, USA. "My other interests besides movies are music (just about anything except rap, big band, and polka), writing poetry, and driving people insane. My first experience in horror that I remember was somewhere in between the ages of 2 and 4 when I saw FIEND WITHOUT A FACE on TV. I was scarred for life, but in a good way. My mainstay is horror, but I love exploitation, some sci-fi and fantasy, even a few chick flicks. And I am the proud owner of Emmett Otter's Jugband Christmas DVD. I'm also working on broadening my horizons by exploring the films of The French New Wave.

# REVIEWS...

## DEAD MEN WALKING
Asylum Home Ent. / 2005
*Review by Mike Haushalter*

**DEAD MEN WALKING** is a bitter jailhouse zombie rampage from The Asylum, written by Mike Watt (**THE RESURRECTION GAME**). Think **28 DAYS LATER** in the slammer and you will have some idea of what to expect from this whiz-bang gut-muncher. Don't expect any subtlety, intelligence or charm however from the collection of cardboard cookie cutter stereotypes that populate **DEAD MEN WALKING** played with uniform stiffness from the entire cast, because there is none to be had they are all simply meat for the beast. The film's storyline doesn't break any new ground either, but from what I have been told it wasn't meant to, it's like the film's characters exists solely as fuel for the zombie carnage. Not that this should come as much as a surprise, the zombie genre is not exactly known for thrilling storylines, snappy dialogue or intriguing characters (but one can always hope). Some of the film's other drawbacks include poor lighting, horrible editing, and ugly murky color.

The film's good points are a brief flash of bare breasts, two truckloads of brutal violence and buckets of grue, gore, and gut munching. This adds up to a fairly average zombie effort (10 years ago I imagine I would have praised **DEAD MEN WALKING** as an above average outing but recent entries to the genre such as the "THE WALKING DEAD," **ZOMBIELAND, SHAUN OF THE DEAD, [REC]** and the **DAWN OF THE DEAD** remake have really raised the bar). All told this should be of interest to zombie fans and a cable staple some time in the future.

## FIVE BLOODY GRAVES / NURSE SHERRI (DOUBLE FEATURE)
*Review by Mike Haushalter*

Hot on the heels of the release of Robert Rodriguez and Quentin Tarantino's **GRINDHOUSE** it seemed that everyone was jumping on the bandwagon with their

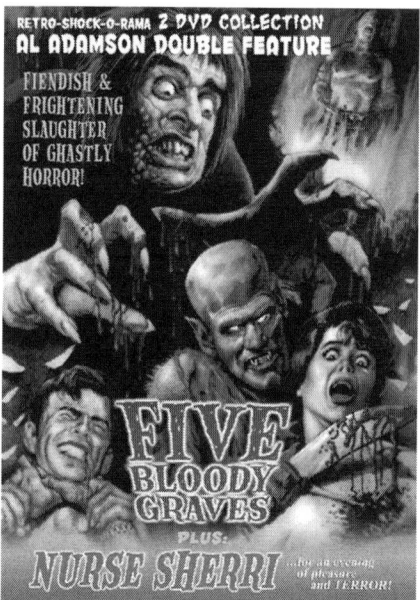

own take on the "grindhouse" double feature experience. Retro Shock-O-Rama Cinema is no exception and they cash in with an Al Adamson twin bill of a drive-in style double feature treat consisting of **FIVE BLOODY GRAVES** and **NURSE SHERRI**. It comes complete with classic animated intermissions and refreshment ads, a handful of Al Adamson trailers and deleted scenes. As a special added treat the set comes with a bonus disc featuring the naughty cut of **NURSE SHERRI**.

### FIVE BLOODY GRAVES

Independent International Pictures / 1970
A renegade tribe of monstrous, murdering, bloodthirsty redskins are on the warpath and every settler will pay with his or her scalp. The lone man who can stop them is Ben Thompson, who rides the desert high plains with Death and Terror as his only companions. Ben seeks vengeance on Satago, the evil Apache chief who butchered his wife on their wedding day, and he teams up with Satago's half-brother to track him down and string him up for the vultures. When the death-dealing duo come upon a wrecked stagecoach carrying prostitutes and a preacher, they battle to keep the survivors alive and in one piece in savage Indian territory.

**FIVE BLOODY GRAVES** is a grim, hard-boiled pulp western, a bitter tale of revenge and resentment so dark that Death himself is the narrator (riding a pale horse no less). Well, okay maybe Death doesn't really show up on his pale horse (a shame really because imagine the imagery would have elevated this film to a cult status) but he is really the narrator.

**FIVE BLOODY GRAVES** is one of the best Al Adamson films I've seen. He make tremendous use of striking outdoor locations and it's familiar story line is bolstered by its clever hook of Death's narration and it's stark manliness coming across as a hybrid mix of the staid American TV western, spaghetti westerns and an Ingmar Bergman film.

The film also boasts from fine performances from its cast. Robert Dix (who also wrote the screenplay) stands out in particular as the cold-blooded hero Ben Thompson. legendary thespian John Carradine also shines in his part as a preacher (just how many preachers has this man played?).

Picture-wise this release is not much to shout about, a pan and scan print which I would best describe as being adequate and made more disappointing when compared with the print quality of the deleted scene which is crisp, clean and letter boxed.

### NURSE SHERRI

Independent International Pictures / 1978
A demented professor of the occult dies on the operating table in this drive-in classic from director Al Adamson. His soul jumps into the curvaceous body of Nurse Sherri (Jill Jacobson) to seek revenge

on those responsible for his death. Soon the possessed lady in white is stalking, seducing and killing for the spirit of the dead professor. Will her fellow nurses remove her curse before she can slay the man she loves?

**NURSE SHERRI** a low rent, Z-grade drive-in film that gets a fresh look from Seduction Cinema in this slick DVD release from their Retro Shock-O-Rama line. If you haven't heard of **NURSE SHERRI** before this it might be because it has been released under many titles over the years including **BLACK VOODOO, BEYOND THE LIVING, HOSPITAL OF HORROR,** and **HANDS OF DEATH**. I first saw this as **BLACK VOODOO** from the Xenon label that they push as a Blaxploitation flick (uh, not quite). This release was a far nicer print than the one I saw before, although Xenon prints do suck out loud. **NURSE SHERRI** is basically a mix of other successful films of the time such as **CANDY STRIPE NURSES, BLAZING STEWARDESSES, ABBY,** and **THE EXORCIST**. Despite it's ragged edges and drive-in origins, Seduction Cinema presents this film with a full complement of extras and features, including an ultra rare never before seen alternate cut of the film. Both cuts have a decent amount of gore, my favorite bit being a dead body in the opening of the film that the professor is trying to bring back to life. This guy is very dead and they let him sit for, like, two more weeks in the desert trying to bring him back to life and he just rots more and more to the point that he's a pack of rats away from being Kenny ("Oh my god! They killed Kenny!"). Other than that, both cuts suffer from being a bit slow moving and padded with an over-abundance of driving scenes. Viewed side by side the release print is the better of the two and is also a bit longer. It's got a stronger story line and a bit of added creepiness. This cut of the film also features a very informative audio commentary by producer Sam Sherman who points out some of the differences between the films and how they came about. The alternate print is a bit shorter and rather scare free but has several sex scenes that were exorcised from the final cut. These scenes do little to add to the story but do add some eye candy and spice to a tame film. In retrospect I believe that they should have kept the sex and shot the new scenes added to the final print to make a more marketable (at the time) trash film, but that's neither here nor there and like they say hindsight is 20/20.

## ROGER CORMAN'S CULT CLASSICS: THE NURSES COLLECTION
*Review by Mike Haushalter*

### PRIVATE DUTY NURSES
New World Pictures / 1971

A trio of ethnically diverse female interns discover love, life and disillusionment in **PRIVATE DUTY NURSES**, the first follow up to New World Pictures' first nurse outing **THE STUDENT NURSES**. Apparently they were still tweaking the nurse franchise recipe when they cooked this one up as it turns out to be an over-flavored, undercooked stew of social and political conscience, feminism, and free love that never really comes to a boil. Early Seventies hot topics such as pollution, drug trafficking, and race relations are all given lip service as is a bit of back from 'Nam bitterness. With so many ingredients thrown into the pot none of them stand out and instead they just muddle the plot.

The film's primary selling point-T&A-doesn't help much either. Sure there is ample flesh on hand to be ogled but frankly it's not very memorable.

The cast is also not very memorable save for a few familiar faces such as Paul Gleason (**THE BREAKFAST CLUB & DOC SAVAGE, MAN OF BRONZE**), and Herbert Jefferson Jr.(Boomer on the original "Battlestar Galactica"), whose smoldering performance as a angry doctor battling against discrimination in the hospital is one of the film's true highlights.

### NIGHT CALL NURSES
New World Pictures / 1972

Another diverse trio of beautiful, free-spirited young women are unleashed upon the medical world in **NIGHT CALL NURSES**, the third outing in New World Pictures' popular and profitable nurses series (do five films make a franchise?).

**NIGHT CALL NURSES** was the debut effort for director Jonathan Kaplan (who would go on to helm drive-in favorites like **THE STUDENT TEACHERS, THE SLAMS,** and **TRUCK TURNER,** and then move on to bigger things like producing television programs like "ER" and "Without a Trace"). He was given almost full reign over the film, along with a $75,000 budget and a 15 day film shoot and he came up with film that takes a Black Power political stand, is chock full of T&A and has imaginative flourishes like a cross dressing knife wielding psycho and a pill popping truckers freak out (wait till you see his disco ball hands!).

Compared to the previous film, **PRIVATE DUTY NURSES** the film, **NIGHT CALL NURSES** delivered a much stronger narrative with a focused political agenda instead of the other film's scattershot hodge-podge of political hot potatoes.

The film's downfall is its leading ladies (Patty Byrne, Alana Stewart, and Mittie Lawrence) who are (IMHO) unmemorable in looks, charm and acting ability (particularly if you happen to watch two or three of these in a row). Another sore point for me was that the acts of political dissent performed by our want-to-be Florence Nightingales at the conclusion of the film led to massive destruction of property and becoming accessories to murder, all of which is completely glazed over and unnoticed in typical movie magic fashion as the film comes to a close.

### THE YOUNG NURSES
New World Pictures / 1973

Wouldn't you know it, just when I thought I had the New World Pictures recipe for success all figured out, along comes **THE YOUNG NURSES**, another tasty dish of T&A nurse-loving that may feature all the staple ingredients that made the first three nurse films so popular-trio of nurses, anti-drug messages, nudity, and feminism, etc...- but they are all served up in a new way that focuses on the day to day drama of working in the the medical field that comes across like a sexy episode of "ER" rather than a smut filled parody of an after-school special.

The first difference from the other nurse outings regular viewers will notice is that the hospital sets are full of extras. The waiting rooms are full, there are patients in beds, surgical teams performing operations, and even paramedics bringing in emergency victims; it's like we are witnessing a "real" hospital rather than an empty hallway and desk masquerading as a hospital.

The next difference is that the film has a more serious tone, no wacky comedy to be found here; instead it seems these nurses really want to make a difference, they are professionals in a serious job and they want to make their world a better place and hold life in a very high regard (this is in sharp contrast to, say, **NIGHT SHIFT NURSES**, where they witness a murder and barely bat an eye).

Even the requisite nudity seems a bit different; in **THE YOUNG NURSES** the actresses seem much more confident and at ease with displaying their skin. Even a few glimpses of full frontal nudity are shown (a rarity in Corman films).

Bolstering these changes is a top flight cast and some surprising guest stars. Jeane Manson is the spunky blonde nurse who has a very hands on bedside manner, Angela Gibbs is the social conscience black nurse opposing the drug trade in her neighborhood, and Ashley Porter is the take change Joanne a nurse unafraid to take risks or break a few rules in the fight to save lives. Ashley Porter delivers her role with a maturity and dynamic missing from most of the other nurses and comes off like a worldly European heroine.

As for guest stars there are Allan Arbus (Sidney the psychiatrist from "M*A*S*H")

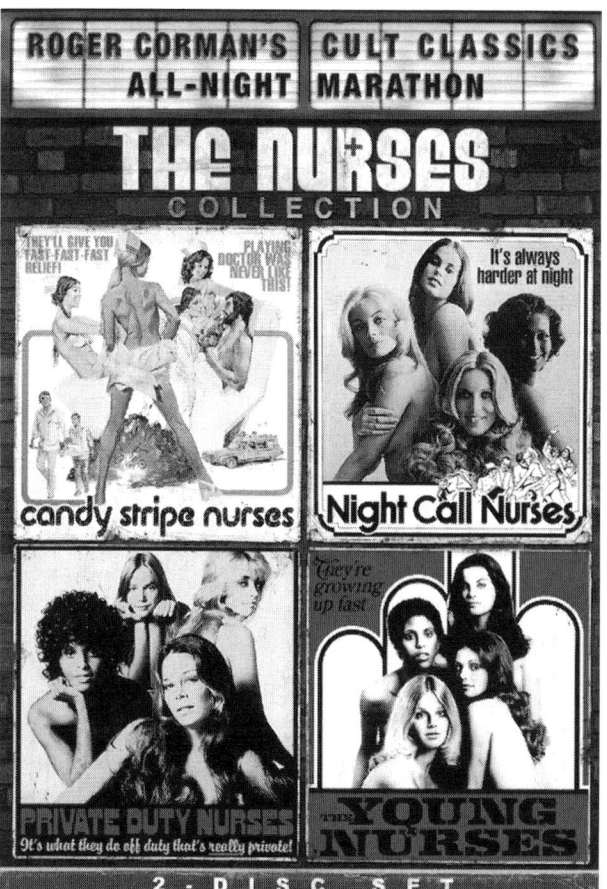

as a head doctor and director Sam Fuller has a weighty cameo as an retired doctor who is not what he seems. There are also a heap of quick cameos by the likes of Dick Miller (as a cop), Sally Kirkland, an uncredited Robert Urich, and Mantan Moreland in his last screen appearance (I was kind of choked up about that I knew he was dead but I didn't realize this was his last film).

## CANDY STRIPE NURSES
New World Pictures / 1974

While New World's 4th film **THE YOUNG NURSES** seemingly catered to the tastes of an audience with more refined palate than the films that preceded it, their fifth and final nurse film **CANDY STRIPE NURSES** would forgo such lofty dramatic aspirations and return to the original recipe of young girls, wacky adventures, after school special drama and heapings of T&A.

**CANDY STRIPE NURSES** is a fun, fast paced film that follows the adventures of a trio of high school girls discovering life, love and lust (like you were expecting anything else); no career minded feminists here just three girls out for a good time.

As far as the cast goes there are not as many famous faces this time out, in fact there are a lot less faces period as this hospital is not full of extras like the last film. Our heroines this time out are Candice Rialson as hot to trot nurse Sandy, María Rojo as the fiery Spanish hot tamale Marisa Valdez, and Robin Mattson as sexy nurse Dianne the smart, caring girl. For my money Robin Mattson is the most stunning starlet of the film and the franchise, she has an outstanding figure that stands out even when compared to the twenty plus other actresses who show off their skin.

You may have noticed that I have not spent much effort talking about the scripts and stories of any of the nurse films that I have just reviewed. Well, let's be honest here, not too many viewers of the Nurse films are in it for the scintillating dialogue and Shakespearean plot lines. These films are about quick thrills, a few laughs and busloads of bare flesh. As such they deliver and frankly I am not sure if you asked me a few months from now which film is which I could even tell you save for **THE YOUNG NURSES** which is about as rewarding storywise as these films come.

## RAGING SHARKS
Nu Image Films / 2005
*Review by Mike Haushalter*

An object from outer space lands in the Bermuda Triangle triggering an unusual phenomenon: a field of magnetic pulses that drive sharks in the area into a frenzy. Do you like shark week on Animal Planet? How about made for SyFy original programing? Do you like gladiator movies? If the answer to those questions is yes, then fire up your bong, turn off your brain and tune in **RAGING SHARKS**, a poor man's combination platter of the **ABYSS** and **DEEP BLUE SEA**. It's the latest in a long line of sharks gone wild efforts of late (and still going strong some 6 of 7 years later).

What's up with all the shark films already? Does anyone know? This is the second shark film directed by Danny Lerner (he would later direct **SHARK IN VENICE**) and the fourth he has

produced. (He is also responsible for **SHARK ATTACK 2**, **SHARK ATTACK 3: MEGALODON**, and **SHARK ZONE**. Today he is producing films such as **CONAN THE BARBARIAN** and **THE EXPENDABLES 2** who'd thunk it.)

## UN ANGELO PER SATANA

*(An Angel For Satan)*
Midnight Choir / 1966
*Review by Danae Dunning*

Sculptor Roberto Merigi (Anthony Steffen) is hired by Count Montebruno (Claudio Gora) to restore a statue fished out of the lake on his estate in 19th Century Italy. This has the villagers up in arms because of a local legend and a 200 year-old curse surrounding it. Things get even more complicated when the Count's niece, Harriet, returns from boarding school in England bearing a striking resemblance to the hated statue. Roberto and Harriet start to fall for each other until she begins acting strangely. She insists on being called Belinda, starts treating both Roberto and her maid, Rita (Ursula Davis) cruelly, and seducing practically every man in the village; setting them against their loved ones and each other. Who is Belinda and what does she want?

Man, am I ever excited. I have been wanting to see **AN ANGEL FOR SATAN** (UN ANGELO PER SATANA)ever since reading about this as a teenager, but thanks to GreenCine.com, this is the first time I've been able to get my hands on it. Was it ever worth the wait. This is Gothic horror at its finest, on par with Hammer Studio's best. Director Camillo Mastrocinque, uses atmosphere to build tension and he and fellow writer Guiseppe Mangione tell an intriguing story that keeps the viewers engaged, and well, what can I say about La Dame Barbara Steele. Just as in Mario Bava's classic **BLACK SUNDAY**, she once again proves that she can go from sweet to malevolent with ease. Even if you're not into Euro horror, I would highly recommend checking this gem out.

## I LUNGHI CAPELLA DELLA MORTE

*(The Long Hair of Death)*
Midnight Choir / 1964
*Review by Danae Dunning*

In 15th Century Europe, Adele Karnstein is falsely accused of witchcraft by Kurt (Weiland Ardisson) in retaliation for spurning his advances. Her oldest daughter, Helen (Barbara Steele) offers herself

to Kurt's father, the Count (Guiliano Raffaelli) in exchange for her mother's life, but to no avail. As Adele burns, she curses the Count's land and descendants, and Helen is tossed over a cliff for her troubles. As Helen's little sister Elisabeth (Halina Zaleswka) grows older, the more she resembles their mother, which unfortunately stirs up Kurt's passions again. As a plague ravages the village and Elisabeth is forced to marry the brute, A mysterious stranger named Mary shows up at the castle. And Mary is the spitting image of Helen...

I wish I could say that I liked this one. As with most Magheriti films, it looks beautiful, but this is so confusing. To start with who exactly is Adele and why was she there in the first place? Was she a servant or relative? Were her daughters wards of the Count? And the revenge is so drawn out, it becomes convoluted. I am reminded of the limerick that asked the question, "Do what and to whom to where?"

You might want to see this for it's classic status alone, but for an Antonio Margheriti film, I would start out with **LA DANZA MACABRA** (CASTLE OF BLOOD) first.

## FROM BEIJING WITH LOVE

*(Gwok chaan Ling Ling Chat)*
Win's Movie Productions Ltd. / 1994
*Review by Bennie Woodell*

**FROM BEIJING WITH LOVE** could quite possibly be Stephen Chow at his very finest. The film is a James Bond parody filled with action, espionage, gadgets, romance, and of course, more than enough slapstick comedy to keep you laughing long after the moment has moved on, this film from beginning to end is a bum rush of sensory overload.

A dinosaur skull is stolen by the Man with the Golden Gun from China, and the Chief of the Police decides to send Ling Ling Chat (Chow) to Hong Kong to capture the Man with the Golden Gun and return the

dinosaur head. Ling Ling Chat goes and meets his aid in Hong Kong, Kam (Anita Yuen), who is acting as a double agent for the Chief of Police, and is supposed to kill Ling Ling Chat, but his charm and wit keep him from death's door.

What really makes **FROM BEIJING WITH LOVE** a fun film to watch, is all the gadgets that are introduced or used. Like, for example, a flashlight that is solar powered and can only work when light is being shone on it, a briefcase that acts as a springboard, or a gun that fires one bullet backwards, then a bullet forwards. These all add to the slapstick elements that made Chow famous, and make wonderful parodies to the gadgets James Bond receives in his films.

The action in the film is also exactly what you can expect from Hong Kong films from the late 80's and early 90's. There's tons of quick cuts, lots of explosions, and super human strength, power, and abilities.

If you're looking for a flick that has everything you could want packed into 84 minutes, **FROM BEIJING WITH LOVE** should be right at the top of your list!

## EL VIOLADOR INFERNAL

*(The Infernal Rapist)*
Esco-Mex / 1988
*Review by Brian Harris*

The vile rapist scum "The Cat" gets the electric chair for his crimes against the community but his great evil has caught the attention of somebody very powerful... Satan herself (Ana Luisa Peluffo)! Seems she wants The Cat to continue his crime spree so she makes him a deal, do her bidding, rape and murder, and in exchange she'll grant him all the pleasure and luxury he desires!

The resurrected rapist immediately sets about his Mistress' bidding and the rape, drugs and carving of 666 commences in full force. The police are baffled, the crimes appear to be by The Cat but they know that's simply not possible as he was executed and declared dead. Is it really The Cat, back from the dead, or is there a copycat killer doing the devil's work? They'll never know unless they rough up some homosexuals, bust some lover's lane humpers and stomp around with mucho macho hard-ons! They know their culprit is bound to turn up and they figure the only way to do that is to catch him in the act

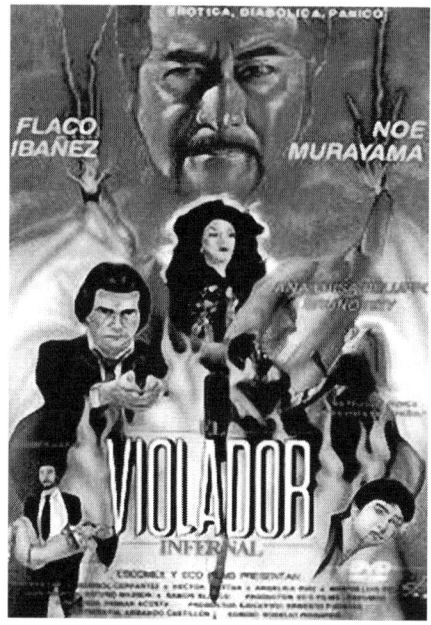

and stop him from carving his diabolical numbers into the flesh of his next victim. Sleaze. By god, so much sleaze. This has heterosexual & homosexual rape by the buttload (wink!), drug use, insane amounts of stabbing and carving and enough he-man bitch-slapping to satisfy the most seasoned misogynist! As **EL VIOLADOR INFERNAL** played out I kept wondering why in hell I'd never seen this film and how in hell I didn't own it! I do now, amigos! Nothing says Mexploitation like Satan and rape! Noé Murayama (**LA LOBA**) was perfect as the debonair Cat, the faces he made during ejaculation were gag-inducing, and Ana Luisa Peluffo (**INTREPIDOS PUNKS**) playing Satan was a stroke of drug-induced insanity. She was hideous to behold (no FX needed) and her constant dramatic entrances, scarf-swinging and cackling had me wondering

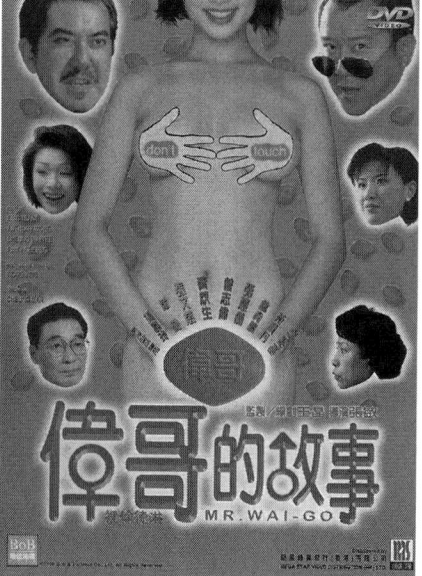

whether director Damián Acosta Esparza was even there for filming!

Yeah, it was that kind of poopy greatness that makes this a must-own film for hardcore exploitation connoisseurs. Grab this film and I promise you'll get to see Princesa Lea's (**EL MACHO BIONICO**) tits. This was a nasty gem.

## MR. WAI GO

*(Wai Goh dik goo si)*
Mega Star / 1999
*Review by Bennie Woodell*

**MR. WAI GO**, which translates to **MR. VIAGRA**, is a Hong Kong comedy written, directed and starring Eric Tsang, who we all know as the triad boss in Infernal Affairs. In terms of Hong Kong comedies, **MR. WAI GO** has a few moments to keep you laughing and wanting more, but that's the problem, you want more because the rest really keeps you looking at the clock on the wall.

The film is basically three short films that just barely intersect. Tsang is having some impotency problems, and discovers that he can get it up by calling the hot widow in town and talking dirty to her. Afterwards, he's ready to attack his wife like an animal in bed. Anthony Wong is Hong Kong's top porn star and is set to film with Japan's top star, but is worried because he can't get it up unless he's watching his wife do housework. He's torn on using Viagra, as he is highly recognizable and doesn't want to lose face to everyone who sees him. Finally, Wong's father is given Viagra as a birthday present as he hasn't had sex with his wife in a long time, she turns him down after taking it, and he saves a young girl from jumping off the roof, and then fights the temptations when she wants to have sex that moment.

Hong Kong films in general never shy away from being absolutely crazy, and **MR. WAI GO** completely follows suit in it's few bursts comedy. The best moments of the film are within Wong's Father's testicles after taking the Viagra. We see his sperm all sitting around playing cards until Viagra shows up, dressed as a superhero all in blue. He gets his troops ready by making them do jumping jacks and other physical activities until they're ready to run down the shaft. Anthony Wong also has a conversation with the most intelligent sperm, who convinces him that he should try Viagra.

7

All in all, those really are the best moments in the film for comedy, as Tsang's story is more of an art house character study. Having seen most of the major, and some of the minor, art films from Hong Kong, Tsang does an excellent job at capturing the character and his innermost thoughts. It is ruined though when it tries to be funny. This story would have worked far better as a dramatic piece.

All in all, just for the few scenes mentioned above, **MR. WAI GO** is definitely worth finding and checking out for any fan of Hong Kong cinema.

# VULCAN
Premiere Entertainment Prod. / 1997
*Review by Brian Harris*

A volcanic eruption disrupts the resting place of a mysterious egg, causing it to hatch a fire-breathing prehistoric bird (think Pterodactyl) dubbed "Vulcan" by a local boy. Quickly forming a bond, the boy and winged companion fly about the Philippines righting wrongs, garnering international attention and dodging treasure-hunting mercs looking to making some big money selling the monstrous creature to the highest bidder. Can an American reporter help the boy to find his long-lost father and the monster a home or will the mercs succeed in stealing a cultural treasure?

Whether the late filmmaker Cirio H. Santiago was trying to illustrate the tragedy of foreigners and their pillaging of the rich history of the Filipino people and land or he was simply looking to create a heartwarming family fantasy film, we may never know. The end result works both ways as it serves to offer a message of hope for an exploited people as well as an entertaining viewing experience. While some may take issue with the hit-or-miss acting, the uneven VFX and the stereotype of white men being sleazy, money-hungry murderers (Vernon Wells, Robert Vaughn & Nick Nicholson), the bottom line is **VULCAN** is a sappy Filipino "Daikaiju" film that's sure to have the kids pretending to fly on giant birds and adults smiling despite themselves. I loved the claymation animation sequences and thought the flight scenes kicked major ass, it was all executed with cheesy goodness.

There isn't a ton of info out there but there appears to be two versions of this film, similar to **GOJIRA** and **GODZILLA, KING OF THE MONSTERS!**, an Americanized cut (**VULCAN**) and a Pinoy release (**ANAK NG BULKAN**). I'd love to see the Pinoy version.

I'm a huge Santiago fan so I wasn't just content to see this, I had to own it as well and I'm betting many of you cult cinema fans will find yourself in a similar position. Grab it now as New Concorde (Corman's distro label) is still offering this thru Amazon and eBay. You can purchase it for about $12, which ain't bad, and if you do a bit of digging you can also find it selling for about $6-10 brand-spankin' new in clamshell case, so tape-humpers and dischoarders can both get their fix! YAY FOR CAPITOLISM! Damn, wait...

# MERMAIDS: THE BODY FOUND
Darlow Smithson Productions / 2011
*Review by Brian Harris*

The mockumentary may not be new to well-versed genre fans but it's easy to see how the uninitiated or gullible may fall for their straight-faced delivery of "facts" that seem positively plausible. Many productions have come down to us thru that years that some, even to this day, will swear they thought were true including **FACES OF DEATH**, **CURSE OF THE BLAIR WITCH** and **DARK SIDE OF THE MOON**. While people often associate the mockumentary sub-genre with something tongue-in-cheek or flat-out comedic, they're often far from it and thoroughly engaging productions of the highest quality. Hell, it was years before I found out the monkey brain and decapitation sequences in **FACES OF DEATH** were staged with actors and SFX!

When my wife mentioned to me that she'd caught a bit of a creepy documentary on Discovery Channel that presented evidence of the existence of honest-to-goodness mermaids, I was intrigued. Don't get me wrong, I know there's no such thing as mermaids but this mockumentary sounded too good to pass up and I was curious to see how they pulled it off. Director Sid Bennett ("I Shouldn't Be Alive") and co-writers Foley and Bhatt ("Pit Boss") deftly weave a story of secret government weapons testing, official denials and international cover-ups around a real unidentified underwater audio anomaly (dubbed "The Bloop") recorded by NOAA (National Oceanic and Atmospheric Administration) in 1997. Without the conspiracy angle you've just got an audio recording and some CG cutaways but with it you're essentially tapping the interest of generations of conspiracy theorists and, for lack of a better word, suckers. You know the types.

Was it successful? Absolutely! **MERMAIDS: THE BODY FOUND** looked like an official nature documentary filled with convincing performances, captivating dramatic reenactments and the above mentioned beautifully rendered CG sequences. Score one for this Animal Planet production and score one for Discovery for picking it up, it was interesting and entertaining. *PATENTLY ABSURD*, but interesting and entertaining nonetheless. And, yes, believe it or not this mockumentary was creepy, though I couldn't say why exactly considering mermaids supposedly live in the *OCEAN* and not under my uncomfortable mattress. Do a Google search on this and you'll be surprised and disappointed to find out how many people believe this was real or want to know if it is. There is indeed one born every minute, no?

*P.T. Barnum exhibited his own mock-monster the "FeJee Mermaid" in 1822, and he labled it "the greatest curiosity in the world". This "mermaid" pre-dated* **MERMAIDS: The BODY FOUND** *by 190 years.*

# KINSKI PAGANINI
Mya / 1989
*Review by Dan Taylor*

You would be hard-pressed to find a more forgiving Klaus Kinski fan than yours truly. Since first discovering "the German Olivier" more than three decades ago thanks to cable viewings of **NOSFERATU: PHANTOM DER NACHT** (1979) and **BUDDY, BUDDY** (1981) the man has become a solid, reliable cinematic presence even when his roles amount to little more than glorified cameos meant to cash in on his name recognition.

Seemingly incapable of "phoning it in," I could always take solace in the fact that even if Kinski was only in a flick for ten or fifteen minutes it was sure to be the best ten or fifteen minutes. Which is what makes **KINSKI PAGANINI** (1989) – finally available domestically in a two-disc special edition courtesy of Mya – all the more disappointing.

The actor's self-professed "dream project," **KINSKI PAGANINI** attempts to tell the tale of Niccolo Paganini, a 19th century violinist and composer whose virtuoso playing and performances paved the way for modern violin technique.

Not that you would get any of that from Kinski's portrayal or the film's "story". Instead, writer/director/star/editor (!) Kinski focuses on Paganini as a proto-rock star, a demonic, seemingly possessed "vampire of the violin" whose fiery performances would make female concertgoers swoon and scream their way to orgasm. (Kinski so identified with the composer that the image of the actor as Paganini was used on the card given to attendees at his memorial service after his death at age 65 in 1991.)

Dribs and drabs of the real Paganini's life make their way into the agonizing voiceovers that dominate the film but the muddled audio and half-hearted dubbing make it hard to decipher more than memorable passages such as "given the chance he would rape every girl he meets!" or "make him repent for his sins and die like a good Christian!". There are also a lot of scenes of carriages. A lot.

Despite his attempts to get the film made for decades, none of the directors Kinski approached with the vehicle would bite. Frequent Kinski collaborator Werner Herzog even went so far as to label the script "unfilmable" and though Kinski would eventually prove him wrong, I don't think Herzog was far off. (Funding for the project was likely secured by Kinski agreeing to appear in other films for producer Augusto Caminito, namely **GRANDI CACCIATORI** (1988) and the much more entertaining **NOSFERATU IN VENICE** (1988).)

Having watched both versions of the film included in the set – an 84 minute "theatrical" cut and Kinski's 98 minute "version originale" – I'll grudgingly admit that Kinski (the actor) comes off better than Kinski (the writer/director/editor). But that is the faintest of praise for a man I strongly believe to be one of cinema's truly great actors.

On screen for the bulk of the flick's excruciating-at-any-length running time, Klaus (the actor) literally throws himself into the role; he stalks, stares, fiddles, gropes, fucks and eats (food, pussy and what appears to be butthole) with wild abandon, all the while sporting an absurd black dye job and muttonchops that make him look more like Mr. Hyde than a legendary composer. A few scenes give him the opportunity to showcase his natural skills, but they're few and far between. Mostly he air plays the violin, walks around in a top hat and bangs/fondles a bevy of comely co-stars (including wife Debora and her titanic sweater puppies). Seriously, **NOSFERATU IN VENICE** is light years more enjoyable and far more deserving of a legitimate release.

Unfortunately, Kinski has nobody to blame but himself for this hot, steamy bowl of incompetence. While the script is nonsense, the editing and camerawork are strictly amateurish. In my efforts to research the man and his career I've talked to multiple co-stars who have lauded his ability to walk onto set and provide constructive criticism that made even the cheapest quickie a better film. How he was incapable of doing that on his one and only directorial effort makes **KINSKI PAGANINI** such a sad, almost unwatchable coda to a legendary career.

The Mya set is essentially a domestic release of the 2003 German PAL/Region 2 release with both versions of the film (1.33:1) in multiple languages as well as deleted and extended scenes, a Cannes press conference, photo gallery and trailer. All that's missing is the original release's German-language booklet.

# THE THEATRE BIZARRE
Severin / 2011
*Review by Dan Taylor*

I came of age as a trash-hound during the 80s and 90s. Forget how it's portrayed in movies and on television, that era ruled. Not only did it feature the last gasp of grindhouses/drive-ins and an explosion of trash cinema zines, but you couldn't swing a re-animated cat without hitting some kind of horror anthology.

Oh sure, horror and sci-fi fans had been blessed with anthologies before... and some damn good ones to boot. TV's earlier eras offered up the likes of Alfred Hitchcock Presents, The Twilight Zone, The Outer Limits, Thriller and (my favorite) Night Gallery, while cinemagoers got the crap scared out of them by visits to **DR. TERROR'S HOUSE OF HORRORS** (1965) and **TALES FROM THE CRYPT/THE VAULT OF HORROR**, a one-two punch of early 70s EC Comics adaptations.

But the 80s and 90s were like a non-stop buffet of anthologized schlock, whether it was pouring forth from the cinema **(TWO EVIL EYES, CREEPSHOW, CREEPSHOW 2, THE OFFSPRING, TWILIGHT ZONE: THE MOVIE, CAT'S EYE)** or, more importantly, your TV screen. No matter what your age or taste, TV had the goods. "Tales from the Crypt", "Tales from the Darkside", "Monsters", "Freddy's Nightmares", "Goosebumps", "The Hitchhiker", "Friday the 13th" and more all spun weekly tales of revenge, horror, evil, and possession, paving the way for what appears to be a new wave of horror anthologies.

**THE THEATRE BIZARRE**, a six-segment feature boasting an all-star cast of trash cinema vets and up and comers, is a worthy entry in this century's tsunami of truncated terror. Loosely connected by a wrap-around story featuring Udo Kier as a creepy mannequin man whose façade slowly erodes to reveal – AIGH! – Udo Kier, BIZARRE's lineup of writers and directors offer up a unique sampling menu of their own. There's an ode to the head-scratching, Lovecraftian-inspired horror flicks of the 80s (Richard Stanley's 'Mother of Toads' featuring Fulci stalwart Catriona MacColl), a gory effects reel steeped in dream-within-a-dream-within-a-dream tropes (Tom Savini's 'Wet Dreams' starring B-scream queen Debbie Rochon), and even a hypnotic (if a bit incongruous) tale of a tragic accident seen through the eyes of a child not much older than my daughter (Douglas Buck's palette-cleansing 'The Accident' which evokes comparisons to a Twin Peaks-era David Lynch).

Of the film's six pack of sinema, however, three tales stand out. **COMBAT SHOCK** director Buddy Giovinazzo's 'I Love You' is a bloody tale of betrayal and suspicion, with Andre Hennicke reminding me of a young Klaus Kinski (though Kinski would have probably blanched at playing someone so paranoid and weak). And despite its itchy-skitchy reliance on eye violence (aka my kryptonite), I'd love to see Karim Hussain's 'Vision Stains' expanded to feature length.

But like a dessert that caps off a delicious meal, David Gregory's 'Sweets' provides a fitting conclusion to the festivities. Packed with eye-popping visuals and a sly, sexy, winking performance from Annette Rothman (who also appeared in the director's excellent feature debut **PLAGUE TOWN**), the segment might make you think twice about going out for cake and coffee after the flick, but it will also send you running to your volumes of Creepy and Eerie that the tale channels.

**THE THEATRE BIZARRE is certainly more hit than miss and** even the weaker segments have their allure. The Severin disc includes commentary from and interviews with the directors in addition to the usual "bonus feature" suspects like trailers and behind the scenes segments, providing plenty of entertainment as we await more anthologies on the horizon like **V/H/S**, **THE ABCs of DEATH** and the Chris Columbus-produced adaptation of Warren Publishing's Creepy.

# RED TO KILL
(Yeuk saat)
Martini Film Company Ltd. / 1994
*Review by Danae Dunning*

Social worker Ms Cheung (Money Lo) oversees the transport of retarded young adult Ming Ming (Lily Chung) to a shelter for developmentally disabled teens after the death of her father. With the exception of the bile spewing neighbors who gather to harass the residents on a daily basis, things seem fine at first. Ming Ming is won over by the other kids, has formed a bond with Ms Cheung, and has a crush on the handsome, kindly director, Mr. Chan (Ben Ng). But the poor girl's affections are misplaced, for her benefactor has a dark secret: He is the "sex lupine" (Don't ask me, I didn't come up with the term.) that has been stalking the neighborhood, infuriated and aroused by the color red. After discovering the creep has been raping Ming Ming, Ms. Chung informs the authorities, but they can't make a case because of the girl's instability, which puts her back into the hands of her tormentor. But our intrepid social worker has plans for the monster...

Wow! I wasn't sure what to expect when I sat down to watch this. I had read reviews of it describing it as "nasty", "repellant", but it's so much more. For something usually classified as exploitative trash, a lot of care went into this. The retarded and autistic people are treated as human beings, and there were heart-wrenching scenes, such as the one where the tearful residents shower a near catatonic Ming Ming with gifts . And the one where Ming Ming is furiously scrubbing herself in the shower and crying pathetically. All of the performances are spot on, but the movie belongs to Ben Ng, who transforms with ease from caring to sadistically nutty. He's an attractive man to boot, but I couldn't enjoy that because his character is such a sicko.

Okay, now for the drawbacks. I'm a little confused as to where the shelter is. Is it in the same building or complex as the complaining neighbors? Across the street?? The subtitles, in a few places, are mistranslated which makes it unintentionally hilarious. ("I mash your penis! I send it to the cook shop!") The score. We have the same saxophone and keyboard riff that has been haunting straight to video **BASIC INSTINCT** rip-offs since the early '90s, and an incredibly annoying pop song that is still echoing through my head. The finale, which involved the normally smart Ms. Chung doing something incredibly dumb, is way over the top and too drawn out to be taken seriously.

Overall, this isn't a bad film, and I hope that eventually it will rise above it's sordid reputation for exposure to people who wouldn't normally watch stuff like this.

## EXTERMINATOR CITY
York Ent. / 2005
*Review by Mike Haushalter*

"It was a dark and stormy night." Thus begins Snoopy's mythical mystery masterpiece (a tribute to anyone suffering from writers block). It's also a pretty valid description of the dystopian future on display in **EXTERMINATOR CITY**.

**EXTERMINATOR CITY** is a hyper-violent, nano-budget, **BLADE RUNNER**-esque body count outing punctuated by over 20 cameos from a virtual who's who list of Spicy Sisters, Web Goddesses, Porn Starlets and Scream Queens (including Julie Strain, Brinke Stevens, Amy Lynn Best, Lilith Stabs, Mistress Persephone, Syn DeVil, Jacklyn Lick, and Taylor Wayne to name but a few). It's a mutant puppet love-child from British director Clive Cohen who has crafted his robot puppet micro-epic with more heart and imagination than any six Hollywood horror films of late and packed it with twice the sleaze to boot.

Speaking of sleaze, **EXTERMINATOR CITY** is loaded with it, offering up an impressive laundry list of exploitation, including over thirty on-screen kills (which has got to be a record for one villain, and I wasn't even counting the robot deaths), eighteen pairs of bare bosoms, and four shower scenes.

## KAALO
Beyond Dreams Entertainment/2010
*Review by Tim Paxton*

After reviewing an odd assortment of earlier made horror gems from India (see page 38), I thought I check out some of the new directors and their films. With little to go on outside of some hyped interviews and questionable reviews I visited my favorite Indian DVD shop online and took a chance.

Wilson Louis's 2010 film **KAALO** garnered a few decent reviews from Indian news sources, so I went out on a limb. The hype and the sleeve art peaked my interest, although I was reluctant to watch the film even though I had been sitting on it for over a month. I had a funny feeling that it was going to turn out to be a major disappointment.

Which it was.

I am more than willing to set aside my western bias in regards to "foreign" horror films. Each culture has its own approach to fright films. Sometimes Westerners only scratch their heads when they are confronted with what another culture finds scary. A fine example would be a Japanese horror film from the 1950s or 1960s. Just why the heck would someone be spooked of a little moth that has flown into the room? I have seen a few Japanese horror films where this has happened. The explanations is that in Japanese folklore a moth is considered the ghost or restless spirit of a lost family member. Sounds silly to a Westerner, but that's the facts (less so now than decades past).

In **KAALO** we have a traditional Indian witch/ghost, a *chudail*, so I was ready for some traditional, albeit updated, Indian horror action. I have been spoiled by watching a lot of older Indian horror films, and when **KAALO** began to play out I began to get a bad feeling about the film.

Had the film stuck to its Indian cinematic roots and had been less tricky with its flashy digital effects, **KAALO** could have been much more successful as a whole. As it stands, only two sequences struck me as original or, at the very least, effective.

**KAALO** was promoted as being original in *one* aspect. Director Wilson Louis was quoted in a glamsham.com online interview in 2011 that he had been, "looking out for a subject that has been never seen on Indian screen so far, Yash Patnaik made my dream come true. We worked on the idea of a creature film but the concept of a day horror came when we were on the film recce." Day horror was the tag line for this film. You get to see the monster in broad daylight. No gloom of night where

any of the creature is hidden from view.

That fact sounded great to me. Some of my favorite Indian monsters are those that have been very visible and very gruesome.

But then no one said that Louis couldn't use excessive POV shots, crappy post-90s Guy Ritchie wacky altered speed/snappy editing, and just lousy cinematography to obscure the titular beastie. He does so much of all that as to make the film almost unwatchable.

A buss load of folks are traveling across the desert toward their destination. They pass by the abandoned village of Kaligarh where, according to the local Rajasrgani folklore, a 600 year old witch lays in wait for young nubile girls. She will take these youngsters and devour them, adding their life force to her own, thus keeping her immortal. As luck would have it the bus has a young girl on board. The witch gets a whiff of her young soul and attacks the bus.

One by one the passengers of the bus are killed off when they attempt to flee the vehicle for the safety of the abandoned village. The usual rabble in these films are dispatched fairly quickly: the four thugs are savagely killed, the two young lovers are run through with a spear while in a wanton embrace, the annoying fashion photographer and his bubble-headed model die in a meaningless manner, and we are eventually left with an old couple who know something about the witch, a mysterious but earnest young man and the girl which, for most of the film, was within easy reach of the witch.

The final showdown takes place within the vicinity of the deserted village of Kaligarth were it is just the young man and the girl against a pissed-off monster.

Pretty hum-drum stuff that has been covered hundreds of times in films going back to the 70s. A monster descends upon a group of tasty humans to picks them off one by one. Standard fare, really. Cookie-cutter. Paint-by-number. Nothing new to note, even the "first ever day horror" bragging rights can only be applied to the Indian cinema that I know of (there are a lot of Western horror films shot in the daylight, not to mention Japanese and Chinese ones).

Approaching this as a purely Indian horror film, **KAALO** *almost* makes the grade. Forty minutes into this 87 minute film we are witness to what should have been the plot's pinnacle turning point. The make or break moment. There is a wonderfully eerie scene where the witch, upon seeing the little girl (sassy young actress Swini Khara) in the bus, *licks the window* nearest to the girl. The sequence goes on for an uncomfortable time and we are witness to extreme close up of the monster's tongue as it glazes the glass. This is the only time that the film found its voice. Here is a horror that has risen from its underground tomb to hungrily search out its next meal of nubile flesh. That single respite of unholy hankering is quickly replaced with more of the duck and cover one comes to expect from hackneyed filmmaking.

The climax of the film comes [spoiler alert] when our hero Sameer (Aditya Shrivastava) is beaten to a pulp by the monster. He is slammed to the ground and left for dead, just barely aware of the girl's pitiful cries for help. Just then, out of nowhere, the soundtrack starts pumping with an inspirational tune about the power of Lord Hanuman the Monkey God. Sameer gains inner strength from Hanuman (he must be a devotee of that god) and attacks the witch with some dynamite he just so happened to have on his person. Calling upon Hanuman was the other moment of pure Indian story-telling. Not unlike the cheap Indian horror films from the 90s, strength through one's faith in a god from the Hindu pantheon is essential when dispatching a demon when all else fails. THAT is what the film should have been, not some lame, far-reaching remake of any number of monster movies from the past thirty years.

**KAALO** is then essentially a cheap horror film in both production and style. Sure, you get to see the monster in broad (way over saturated) daylight. And, yes, the creature is more man-in-a-suit than computer graphics (a welcomed sight despite the rest of the film's faults), BUT all that does not make a good monster or horror movie. If you really want to make a good Indian horror film, Mr. Louis, don't waste your time with pseudo-snazzy camera work and cheap digital effects. You had a cool monster you should have made something out of it.

# THE FILMS OF PAUL KENER

*Reviewed by Douglas Waltz*

This should be relatively easy as the mysterious Paul Kener only made two films; Wendigo and Savage Water. With that

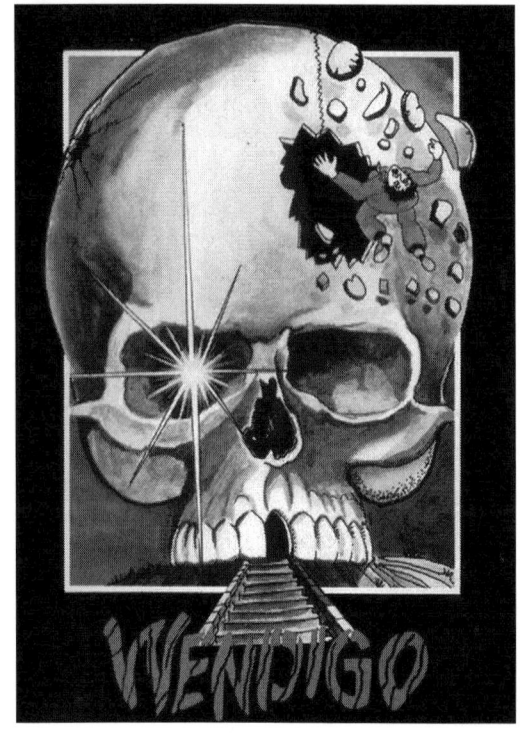

12

kind of filmography we can cover each film, although they have a lot in common.

## WENDIGO (1978)

Frank Benson (Ron Berger) and his lovely wife Connie (Carole Cocherelle) are on their honeymoon. What a better way to celebrate than go on a moose hunt. They bring along their photographer friend Eric Jennings (Cameron Garnick) and head for the untamed North. Of course, the only way to get there is by helicopter so with Mike Coglan (Robert Steffen) as their ex Vietnam pilot they make their way to camp.

Greeted by their crusty, French-Canadian guide Defago (Van Washburn Jr.) and his Indian friend, Billy (Victor Lawrence), the group gets ready to go on the hunt.

But something lurks in the island close to the mainland. Something whispered about by the natives, like Billy.

The demon known as Wendigo.

When Mike attempts to leave his helicopter is tossed through the air and explodes. Mike is barely able to escape into the chilly water with a few cuts and bumps. Now they are stuck until someone comes to find out where Mike made off to. Mike and Eric are sure that the island holds more than Moose. They have heard of a treasure. And treasure holds more of an allure than the threat of some mythological monster whispered throughout the frozen North.

**WENDIGO** is the first film that Paul Kener made. It is obvious that the people in it and the people behind the camera are all the outdoors type. They handle canoes, horses, helicopters like it was second nature. This, unfortunately, does not make them good actors. Kener tries to spice things up with the lovely Carole Cocherelle, but when all we see is her naked back, well it just isn't the same.

The amazing thing about **WENDIGO** is it comes across as an Andy Milligan film if Andy was the outdoorsy type. The look of the film and the cinematography, which is really quite good, lets you forgive the acting chops of this particular crew.

The beast is hardly shown which adds more suspense to the film.

But, there's this one amazing shot.

When they are being chased by the Wendigo, Eric is in a canoe by himself. Suddenly, he is lifted into the air and then his body explodes in a fiery ball of death. I would assume they used the helicopter to achieve this, but it is so damned seamless it looks like Eric is magically lifted into the air. It works. A lot of this works and when you add the Milligan feel to the mix you have a film that is captivating and near impossible to push the pause button.

A final thing I really need to mention about **WENDIGO** is the lead guide Defago. Throughout the film he uses the worst French accent I have ever heard. He makes Pepe LePew sound fluent. I do give him credit that he never breaks character and the accent stays as horrible as something that would be in a bad high school play.

**SAVAGE WATER** is another thing altogether. It feels like this one was made first. It deals with a tourist group of river rafters. There is all creed and color in the mix and they are just taking a little jaunt down the Colorado River through the Grand Canyon.

Except someone is killing them off one at a time.

I appreciate what must have been a logistical nightmare with this large a cast of amateurs and setting it on the water and, as **WENDIGO**, the cinematography is well done.

But, it feels like a home movie where they decided to throw in a plot. The only problem is that whoever threw in the plot throws like a limp wristed girl and it just doesn't stick. The person they accuse of being the killer makes no sense and the twist ending makes more sense of the whole thing, but you get it way before it

French VHS art for **SAVAGE WATER**

ever happens.

There is one aspect of this film that makes it slightly important. In no way is it as good as **WENDIGO**, but it has this one thing.

You see, **WENDIGO** takes place up North and people are dressed for hunting. Hunting styles never change all that much. Lots of plaid and tan goes a long way. But, **SAVAGE WATER** is tourists straight from the late seventies. The decade was almost over and the clothing choices are such a time capsule. When the leader of the rafting expedition and his two comrades are discussing what route they are taking in denim shorts that would put Daisy Duke to shame it is a laugh out loud moment. The clothes show the time period and for that it has a little worth.

After that Paul Kener just stopped making movies. Better people than I have tried to track him down to no avail. I prefer to think that he just saw it wasn't worth his time when there was so much camping, rafting and hunting left to do. Paul Kener disappeared back into his rugged outdoor world and left us with these two bizarre testaments of a man with a dream of making cinema.

If only he had made more.

And, I think that Kener missed his calling as a product placement man. There is a scene where Connie is in her tent and she's reading a novel titled Savage Water. It even says on the back cover that it is now a thrilling motion picture. If only it was true.

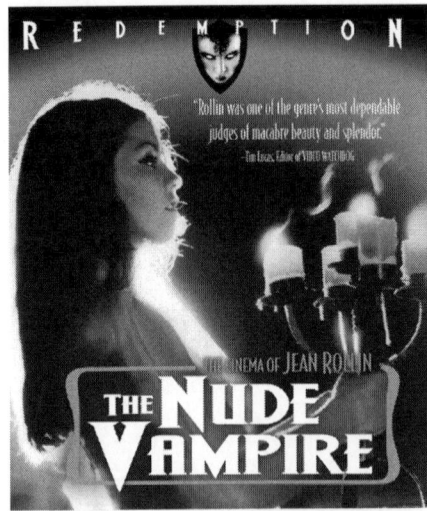
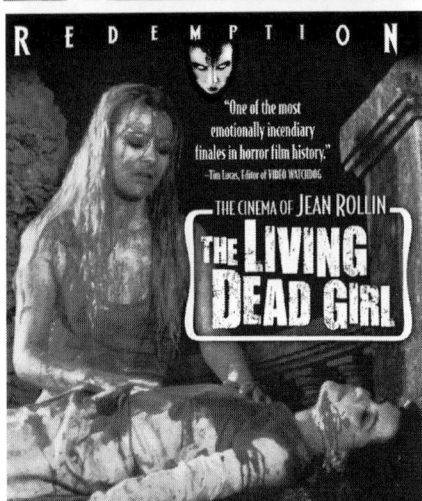

# TROIS FILMS DE JEAN ROLLIN

*Reviews by Danae Dunning*

## LA VAMPIRE NUE
(The Nude Vampire)
Redemption Films / 1970

A rich industrialist, Radamante (Marice Lematre) presides over a suicide cult while keeping a mysterious woman (Caroline Cartier) prisoner believing her blood holds the secret to immortality. Meanwhile, His son, Pierre (Olivier Martin) is highly suspicious and launches a campaign to find out what's going on.

Er, I think. To be honest with you, I had to go to IMDb (Internet Movie Database), because I could not assemble a coherent plot even thought I just watched it. If you are curious about Jean Rollin, trust me, his earlier films are not the best place to start. Just a series of Gothic scenery, and beautiful often naked, women held together vaguely by a premise. Surreal is an understatement, Especially for LA VAMPIRE NUE. Martin, the director's half brother, makes an attractive and personable hero, and Cartier does what she can with her limited role, but I really can only recommend this for fans of the truly bizarre.

## REQUIEM FOR A VAMPIRE
Redemption Films / 1971

Two young women on the lam hole up in graveyard, stumble on a Gothic castle, and get indoctrinated into a cult of vampires.

Yep. That's it. Once again, we have a the barest thread of a plot as an excuse to weave together images of beautiful women being ravished in a Gothic castle, including a shot of a vampire bat going where no vampire bat, or any other animal, should go. (Ouch) Rollin claimed that he didn't want the sex, but the producers insisted. Without it, though, there is no way to fill the 86 minute running time, which is stretched out as it is.

## THE LIVING DEAD GIRL
(La morte vivante)
Redemption Films / 1982

Helene (Marina Pierro) is incredibly shocked to receive a phone call from her frightened childhood friend Catherine (Blanchard), who happens to be recently deceased. Apparently, some thieves broke

---

For more information on Jean Rollin, check out the classic 1996 issue of the MONSTER! INTERNATIONAL #4/HIGHBALL: #2 **Special Double Issue** for sale though the Weng's Chop Bookshelf on page 52. Highball Cover shown below, M!I cover shown on the order page.

into the tomb located below Catherine's family home, and spilled some toxic waste, which not only reanimates her, but leaves her with an insatiable thirst for blood.

Yes, this is your standard Jean Rollin: lush production values and beautiful, often naked women. But this has an actual story. And a good one at that, with characters you can emotionally invest in. You began to hate the selfish Helene, who will do anything to keep her friend in some semblance of life, and your heart breaks for Catherine, because the more blood she consumes the more aware she becomes of what she is and what she must do. It becomes quite clear who the actual monster is.

# MIL SEXOS TIENE LA NOCHE
Golden Films Internacional S.A / 1984
*Reviewed by Timothy Paxton*

I have enjoyed the films of Spanish film director Jesus Franco since I was teen, when I appreciated that he put a mustache on Christopher Lee in **COUNT DRACULA** (1969). It's been over 30 years since that fateful Saturday afternoon viewing and, despite drooling over the occasional review in the magazine "Castle of Frankenstein", it was tough finding any of his films to watch (although his 1964 film **DR. ORLOFF'S MONSTER** played a few time on TV during that time period). That was the situation until VHS rentals took off in the early 1980s.

The mid to late 1980s was when the sell-thru market started pumping out budget bargin bin titles. It was also when public domain companies began offering Franco's older titles from the 1960s (**AWFUL DR. ORLOF**, **ATTACK OF THE ROBOTS**, and **THE DIABOLICAL DR. Z**) and quasi-legit companies releasing films from the 1970s (**DEMONIAC**, **THE SCREAMING DEAD**, **BLOODY MOON**, **DRACULA**, and **MANHUNTER**). I began watching and cataloging Franco's work.

In the late 80s I stumbled upon the VHS Private Screenings of **THE LOVES OF IRINA**, the softcore English-language edit of Franco's 1973 erotic horror film **THE FEMALE VAMPIRE**. The film features the gorgeous Lina Romay in all her naked glory. She is the lonely vampire Countess Irina Karlstein who hungers for love as much as she does for sex and blood. It is my essential Romay film followed by **SHINING SEX** (1977), **ROLLS-ROYCE BABY** (1975), **DORIANA GRAY** (1976), **THE TENDER AND PERVERSE EMANUELLE** (1973), and **LORNA THE EXORCIST** (1974).

There are so many films by Franco with Romay that you can get lost in what you've seen and not seen. These are films that I've wanted to see for years, or had at one time on VHS but no longer possess. For this review I'll lay a pretty cool one on you.

**MIL SEXOS TIENE LA NOCHE** ("Night Has A Thousand Sexes") is one of those mysterious films by Jess Franco which is steeped in lovely cinematography, stunning women, and a plot that is more poetry than prose. The film is also a horror-tinged noire for want of a better description. The film features the lovely Lina as Irina, a woman who possesses clairvoyant abilities and works in a night club act with her lame boyfriend Fabián (Daniel Katz). Their mind-reading act is very popular, but Irina is plagued by overtly erotic dreams and violent nightmares of death and murder.

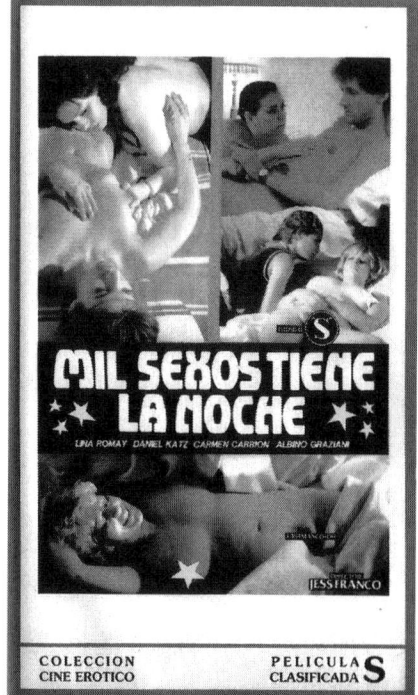

Spanish VHS box art.

Sex and death... a very popular theme explored with voyeuristic abandon by the director. And I am not one to complain, as I drink up every intoxicating scene and stumble about in a cinematic stupor. This is essential Franco.

However, this film is not perfect. As lovely as it is to watch, **MIL SEXOS TIENE LA NOCHE** doesn't come close to some of the Franco/Romay's earlier efforts mentioned earlier. Franco's otherwise dark soundtrack (under the pseudonym Pablo Villa) is punctuated by some pretty piss-poor jazzy pop numbers, which for the most part, totally destroy any sense of mood. Whereas the Franco/Daniel White score for **LOVES OF IRINA** felt as if it was intrinsically valuable to the filmmaking, these seemingly random night club jazz tracks are more annoying than anything else. But more about "Irina's Love Theme" a little later.

Another distraction is actor Katz who starred in a few other Franco films from this time period (**HISTORIA SEXUAL**

*Not the actual cover of the MacDonald book that appeared in the film, but you get the general idea, as does Irina!*

15

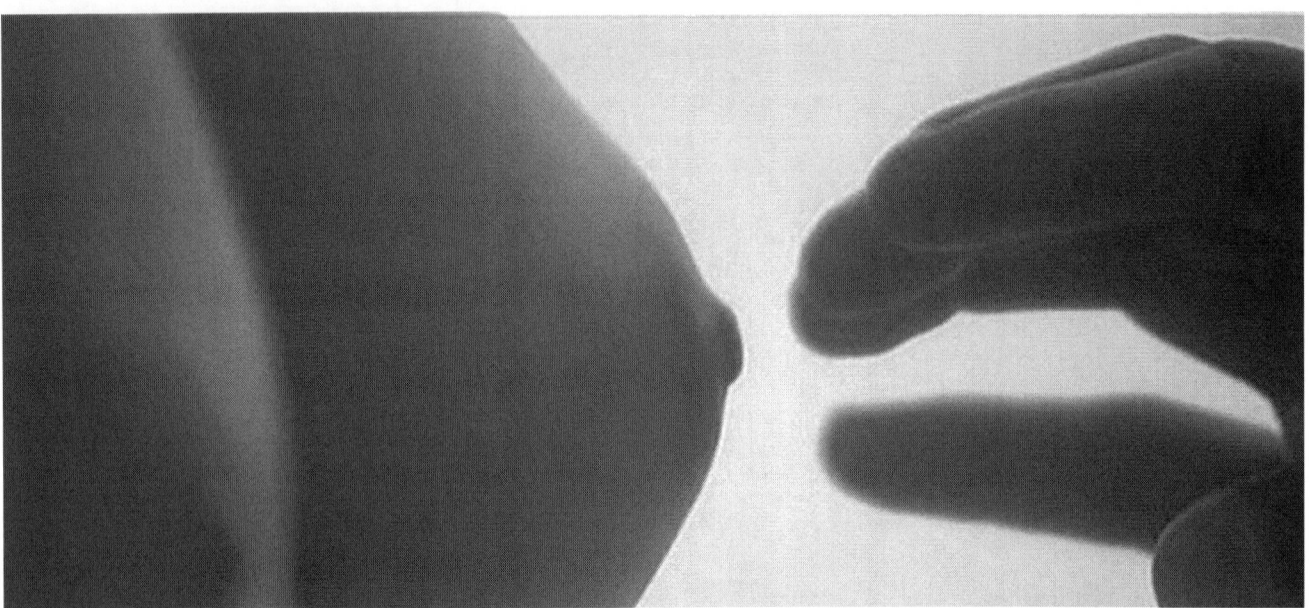

DE O, ESMERALDA BAY, and BLOOD ON MY SHOE) as well as starring in José Ramón Larraz's REST IN PIECES (1987). He is rather boring as an actor. The film is pretty much Lina's baby throughout.

As the plot progresses it is apparent that Fabián is using Irina in a rather twisted form of revenge. Is Irina dreaming death into existence as much as she is with her erotic liaisons? Or is it the Ross MacDonald paper back "The Ivory Grin" influencing her dreams? Who knows, but I love that a vintage 1950s detective novel is included in the film (well, an 80s reprint of the 1952 novel). I'm sure that Franco is a fan of MacDonald's work, as those novels tend to be incredible. Could this scene where Irina absently picks up a copy of MacDonald's book only to glance at it. On the cover a woman's mouth clenches a blood scalpel; maybe Franco's tribute to the author who died in 1983? Could be, the Franco clearly loves the genre.

Irina's world begins to crumble around her as her shit of a boyfriend abuses her metal powers, turning her into a killing machine. In desperation she visits a psychiatrist (Franco in a cameo) to confess her violent dreams. She wrongly assumes that the doctor's indifference means he's not paying attention to her. (Luckily for her this proves wrong.) Afterwards she wanders the lush landscape (Costa del Sol, Málaga, Andalucía, Spain to be exact), until she encounters a young man. In the film's most erotic sequence, Irina and the young man make love. Sadly, Irina gets the mental order to kill, and stabs her lover to death in mid fellatio. She staggers back to Fabián, only to find that he has other plans for her.

Sex and death have always been an intricate part of Franco's vision. This theme is so common a thread in his filmography that the man can't help but reference earlier works. Sometimes it is the use of a name, as with Orlof (or Orloff), Morpho, Johnson, and in this case Irina. In fact, nods to LOVES OF IRINA not only surfaces in our heroine's name, but in the death by blowjob sequence, and that the love theme from the 1973 film filters in during that scene's love-making.

Franco also tends to revisit, rework, and revamp earlier films. You could say that MIL SEXOS TIENE LA NOCHE is a very distant cousin to his original erotic masterpiece from the 1960s MISS MUERTES (aka THE DIABOLICAL DR. Z). The object of possession, obsession, death and night club scenes permeates this and many of this films.

Until recently MIL SEXOS TIENE LA NOCHE had only been available on VHS from the late 1980s. Before that it was an obscure, little seen film that was based on an equally rarer 1970 film called LES CAUCHEMARS NAISSENT LA NUIT. (which has only recently been uncovered and released on UK DVD under the title NIGHTMARES COME AT NIGHT). The plot is very similar and stars Diana Lorys and Colette Giacobine, with Lory's character being the one having the brutal nightmares. That film also stars Franco regulars Jack Taylor, Paul Muller, and Soledad Miranda in a small role. This film (and another obscurity called SEX CHARADE, which looks to have shared identical cast and crew, also from 1970), shortly before Miranda's pivotal role as Condesa Oskudar in the extremely popular LOS VAMPYROS LESBOS stamped her as the ultimate Franco fetish icon.

As luck would have it LES CAUCHEMARS NAISSENT LA NUIT was revamped a few years later for a Dr. Orloff project called the THE SINISTER EYES OF DOCTOR ORLOFF (now available thru Intervision Picture Corp., in Spanish and subtitled in English). I for one don't mind when Franco revisits old haunts. Some of his best films from the 1980s, like MIL SEXOS TIENE LA NOCHE, are those that have classic characters from the past woven into their plots. EL SINIESTRO DR. ORLOFF (1982), REVENGE IN THE HOUSE OF USHER (1983), and FACELESS (1988) all take cues from Franco's classic THE AWFUL DR. ORLOF from 1964 and run with it.

*It would seem that sex, death and rebirth may well be part of the director's personal process of renewal. The sad death of Ms. Romay earlier this year will no doubt have a profound effect on Franco. Although he still has films in the works, Lina was his muse, and some of his most effective and memorable films starred her. R.I.P. Lina Romay, you are missed.*

# I WANT THIS POOL DRAINED!
# INTERVIEW WITH YAPHET KOTTO

Article & Interview by Phillip Escott

He's worked with some of the biggest names in Hollywood, from the likes of Ridley Scott, Arnold Schwarzenegger and Tommy Lee Jones to Richard Pryor, Isaac Hayes and Gary Busey to mention but a few, and has had a productive 50 year career in showbiz. Yet Yaphet Frederick Kotto remains a cult figure, adored by fans of B-movies the world over, whilst rejected by the mainstream institutions that run the industry; only finding recognition for his work in television with a number of Emmy nominations, but no wins.

I've been an admirer of Yaphet's work for some time, like many, his role as Parker in Alien was my introduction to his filmography and to this day I still think he's the unsung hero of the film. I can respect a man who's looking to get paid for his labour, but have always been left cold by Ripley's blind, business-minded respect for 'the company' throughout the film; Parker at least questioned their orders and demands extra credits for work he's not actually contracted to do!

Yaphet also battled another monster that haunted my childhood dreams, one Freddy Krueger, in **A NIGHTMARE ON ELM STREET 6: FREDDY'S DEAD**: which really would have benefited with more Kotto on screen and less Goo Goo Dolls on the soundtrack, but I digress. Outside of these big studio pictures are a wealth of fantastic movies that feature

U.K. poster for **BONE**

Yaphet Kotto more heavily, and these are the films I urge you to seek out, as fun as a film like **LIVE AND LET DIE** is, it doesn't come close to these:

# BONE (1972)

(aka **BEVERLY HILLS NIGHTMARE, DIAL RAT FOR TERROR** & **HOUSEWIFE**)

The directorial debut of the hugely prolific Larry Cohen also happens to be his best. Abandon all political correctness; this is Grindhouse at its most fiercely intellectual and blinding in its blacker-than-black humour. Think **FIGHT FOR YOUR LIFE**… with more brain, and even bigger balls, and you're on the right track. Kotto is brilliant in the titular role, a thug who's been rendered impotent by the dissolve of the 'Nigger mystique' due to the acceptance of his race by the snobby middle-class white folk. To give away any more would ruin the surprise, this is classic material that all fans of cinema need to seek out.

# BLUE COLLAR (1978)

Paul Schrader's directorial debut is a crushing examination of the working class lives of three workers at an automobile factory in Michigan and a scathing attack on the unions who are supposedly out to protect them. The movie is well known for the trouble on-set between the three leads, a famous incident of Richard Pryor threatening Schrader with a gun being just one, however watching the movie you would never have known. Richard Pryor is excellent as family man Zeke and is backed-up with stellar performances by both Harvey Keitel and Yaphet Kotto, as Jerry and Smokey respectively. Paul Schrader apparently suffered from an on-set mental breakdown due to all the tension, but the finished product was worth suffering for; this is one of America's masterpieces of 70's cinema that remains criminally underrated.

# EYE OF THE TIGER (1986)

Now, you might be wondering why this would be on the list when there are movies like **ACROSS 110TH STREET, ALIEN, LIVE AND LET DIE, DRUM, THE RUNNING MAN, TRUCK TURNER** and many other superior films to choose from in Kotto's filmography, but the truth is… they just aren't as fun as this! Now, before Village Roadshow made mega-hits like **THE MATRIX** and Oscar-winners like **TRAINING DAY**, they made films like Eye of the Tiger! A rip-roaring tale of revenge that sees Gary Busey and Yaphet Koto team-up in a Riggs and Murtaugh fashion to take on a whole gang of motorcycle-riding cocaine pushers (led by head villain 'Blade'!) with brute force, and a bomb-dropping crop-duster aeroplane, after the brutal murder of Busey's wife! All while Survivor's classic **EYE OF THE TIGER** plays out over the soundtrack! It's all incredibly ridiculous in execution and exceptionally cheesy but, damn it all to hell; it's a tonne of fun and that's why **EYE OF THE TIGER** deserves to make the list.

I was lucky enough, and honoured, to get some questions in to Yaphet recently to discuss some of these films as well as others in his long, productive career. Needless to say he was as raw and honest in his responses as he is on screen.

*It's well known that you had a tough upbringing in the Bronx; do you think this played a part in you wanting to be an actor? A sort of escape, if you will?*

My desire to be an actor came as a result of my need to express my inner person in an area that found black Jews unacceptable. My family sent me to all-Catholic schools and I always found myself not joining in their prayers, unwillingly attending mass and being quiet when the references of Jesus were made in my hearing and not speaking out for fear it would draw resentment from the Monks or Nuns who taught the class.

Acting gave me the ability to speak out in catholic school; especially I remember being spanked with a bamboo stick for saying that Jesus was our Rabbi and not God. I've never forgiven the catholic schools for all the whippings they put on me.

*Growing up with access to 42nd Street you must have seen some wild shit, can you remember any particular events you could share with us.*

I didn't grow up around 42nd Street, I was born in Harlem and later we moved to the Bronx and the Soundview projects. One afternoon after going to a place in lower Manhattan "Warren Street' to buy a part time job, I met with no success and took the train ride back up to Times Square. I wandered around and looked at all the porno theatres and luncheon walk-ins and considered buying a coke and a frankfurter when I saw the advertising for a movie "On the Waterfront." Well, I walked into that theatre to see the film and when I walked out my entire life was changed. I swore then I was going to become an actor.

*During its golden era, you were in some of the greatest Blaxploitation films produced. With the resurgence in the genre, thanks to **BLACK DYNAMITE** and soon with Quentin Tarantino's **DJANGO: UNCHAINED**, what are your memories on that movement and your involvement with it?*

Look, I did one movie I considered to be "Blaxploitation" and Isaac Hayes, my then friend talked me into it, what is more important is that a movie I made **THE LIBERATION OF LORD BYRON JONES** directed by William Wyler depicted a black man killing a white man on screen. It had never been done in Hollywood; it ended the **LILIES OF THE FIELDS** era and created a new kind of black anti-hero. That one film changed all of Hollywood, as did **LIVE AND LET DIE** and **ALIEN**, because they too were first and changed the image of black men on screen. My memories of that era for movies like **DRUM** and **MANDINGO** should have expired. Forever! I don't get any credit for it, because a lot of bullshit people would like to keep me their little secret. Therefore no NAACP image award for Yaphet Kotto. Who's that? Oh, he's that black Jew who just happened to turn the whole fucking industry around. Let's forget him! Let's make NIGGER: UNCHAINED, so we can win an academy award and make everyone cry about what they did to us. Bullshit!

We now have a black President in the White House; we don't need another slave picture to remind us of what? It's hypocritical to keep going back in history showing us as slaves and crying over what the 'White Man' did to us. It's over! We need to stop crying and stop pointing fingers at the white man! Will I see that day hell no, not while there's awards to be won.

*You've directed numerous theatre plays, but only one movie to date, 1972's **THE LIMIT**; how was the experience and why didn't you continue to direct film after it?*

All that I've done, the film I produced, the writing I did for "Homicide", (which by the way changed everything in television) has prepared me to one day direct and I'm just about ready to start directing and producing, two major film companies are presently talking to me about joining them on an executive level and I'm trying to be able to sort out sitting behind a desk and directing at the same time.

*You were involved in one of the greatest TV shows ever created, "Homicide: Life on the Street". How did you find it developing a character like 'Gee' Giardello over the years, as opposed to just a few months for a movie? Especially seeing as he's based on a real person.*

I couldn't have developed Gee without the help of Tom Fontana and Barry Levinson, Fontana is a brilliant writer and I don't have to say much to you about Levinson. An actor's performance is always teamwork between a number of people and I was lucky enough to have Fontana and Levinson. God bless them both.

*My personal favourite of your films is **BONE** (aka **DIAL RAT FOR TERROR**), how did you come about getting involved with Larry Cohen and the project?*

**BONE** is my favourite too. Now, is the time to re-create that character, after all these years, now I understand that script. I wish I could do it all over again, it was ahead of its time, and it scared the shit out of a lot of people. I forget how I met Larry, through a mutual friend or an agent, I can't remember, but it was right after a year of starring as Jack Johnson on Broadway and I was ready for it. **BONE** is my favourite character.

*You got to star along side many, many actors over the years, but not as many who are as... charismatic as Gary Busey. You filmed **EYE OF THE TIGER** with him in 1986, which is a riot, how did you find working alongside him?*

Gary Busey is insane. Period.

**19**

*You also got to act alongside my favourite comedian, Richard Pryor, in what is arguably his greatest performance on* **BLUE COLLAR***. It must have been quite the experience?*

I have so much respect for Richard. He was one of the actors who broke down the door of racism for us in this business. He did it and kept his sense of humour, many of the years and hardships he went through had its toll on his personal life, so I understood where he was coming from when he suffered. He was one of our pioneers and if it weren't for men like he and Sidney Poitier, there would be no Yaphet Kotto or Denzel Washington, Morgan Freeman or Danny Glover, those guys made it possible for us all.

*How was it working with one of Hollywood's great screenwriters, Paul Schrader, on that project?*

Paul Schrader is a genius. Just read some of his scripts. Don't just watch his movies, read his scripts and drink in the imagery he's able to convey in sentence or a piece of dialogue, reflections that a camera would never be able to pick up. I can't wait to read a book he writes, he reminds me of the late Budd Schulberg and his simple descriptions of characters and places always bring you right in. I'm glad to have known them both.

*Ridley Scott has finally released* **PROMETHEUS***, as a sci-fi fan and one of the actors in the original* **ALIEN***, what are your thoughts on his latest entry in the franchise?*

I didn't like **PROMETHEUS** for a sundry of reasons that are too long to mention. There isn't enough room on the internet.

*Are there any projects you're working on at the moment we should be looking out for?*

I'm getting about two or three offers a month about all the things I've done before so I'm writing a book 'Yaphet Kotto's Alien Diary' and like I say, don't be surprised to hear that I'm now an executive at [Undisclosed] studios with a directing deal.

With writer. actor, director Cornel Wilde from **SHARKS' TREASURE** (1975)

**We here at Weng's Chop would like to thank Yaphet for his time and wish him every success with all future endeavours.**

With Pam Grier from **FRIDAY FOSTER** (1975)

# KILLER SHREW FACTS

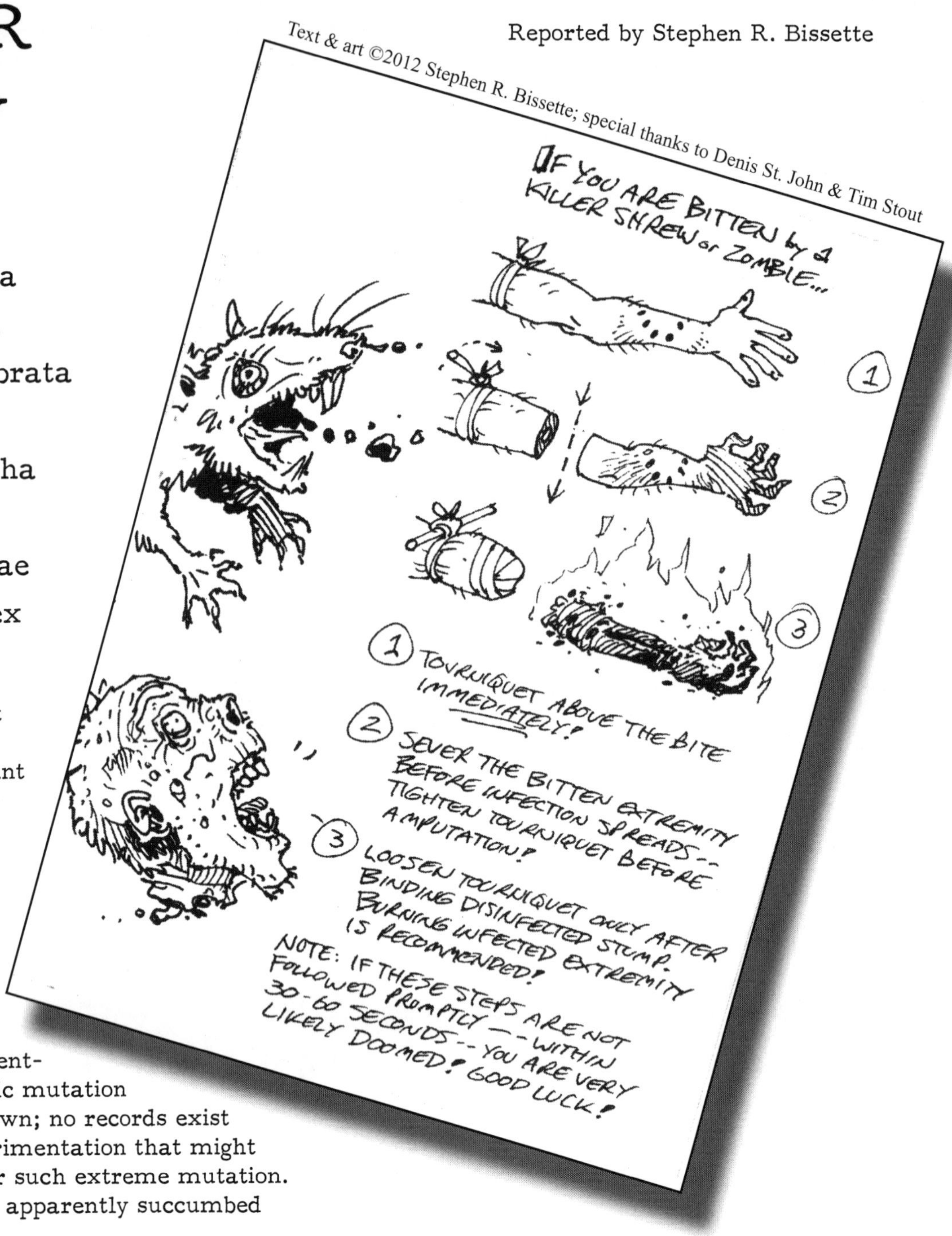

Kingdom: Animalia
Phylum: Chordata
Subphylum: Vertebrata
Class: Mammalia
Order: Soricomorpha
Family: Soricidae
Subfamily: Soricinae
Species: Blarina rex

Reported by Stephen R. Bissette

Text & art ©2012 Stephen R. Bissette; special thanks to Denis St. John & Tim Stout

*[Handwritten illustration with instructions:]*

**IF YOU ARE BITTEN by a KILLER SHREW or ZOMBIE...**

1. TOURNIQUET ABOVE THE BITE IMMEDIATELY!
2. SEVER THE BITTEN EXTREMITY BEFORE INFECTION SPREADS -- TIGHTEN TOURNIQUET BEFORE AMPUTATION!
3. LOOSEN TOURNIQUET ONLY AFTER BINDING DISINFECTED STUMP. BURNING INFECTED EXTREMITY IS RECOMMENDED!

NOTE: IF THESE STEPS ARE NOT FOLLOWED PROMPTLY -- WITHIN 30-60 SECONDS -- YOU ARE VERY LIKELY DOOMED! GOOD LUCK!

---

Though scientists have long known of the Giant Mexican Shrew (Genus Megasorex) and the Giant Elephant Shrew (Rhynchocyon petersi), the so-called 'Killer Shrew' (Blarina rex) seems to be an anamoly particular to only two known island habitats off the coast of Texas. The existing populations were apparently the result of dramatic mutation caused by agents unknown; no records exist of any authorized experimentation that might have been a catalyst for such extreme mutation. Both island populations apparently succumbed to species cannibalism.

As with the common North American shrew species found in nearly all terrestrial habitats, it appeared the Killer Shrew populations favored damp brushy woodlands, bushy bogs and marshes, and weedy and bushy borders of fields. Evidence indicates they sought shelter in standing barns, cellars and sheds on both islands during inclimate weather, surviving at least four hurricanes. Investigation of the islands indicated the shrews had constructed elaborate subterranean runways between man-made shelters, and nests were found in tunnels and under larger logs and rocks.

Blarina rex carcasses and remains indicate the species reached a total body length, from tip of the nose to tip of the tail, from 1000 to 1500 mm in males, and 870 to 1370 mm in females. Tail length ranges between 600 to 825 mm. Males weighed from 30 to 80 kg, with an average of 55 kg, females from 23 to 55 kg, with an average of 45 kg. Height (measured from base of paws to shoulder) generally ranged from 60 to 90 cm.. Males were slightly larger than females, especially in the skulls. The fur was velvety and soft, and the color almost uniformly brown-gray, with the underparts being only slightly paler. For the duration of their existence, Blarina rex were robust, the snout longer and heavier than that of other shrews, the tail long, the eyes small, and the ears almost completely hidden by the fur.

Some key physical features:
endothermic ; bilateral symmetry .

Sexual dimorphism: male larger.

Reproduction:

Breeding interval
Female 'Killer Shrews' may have had multiple litters throughout the warm months of the year, depending on food availability.

Breeding season
The breeding season lasted from March through September.

Number of offspring
3 to 10; avg. 6

Gestation period
22 days (high)

Time to weaning
20 days (low)

Age at sexual or reproductive maturity (female and male)
65 days (average)

Elaborate mating nests were found on both islands, built out of shredded grass or leaves and placed in deep tunnels or under logs and rocks. The breeding season extended from early spring to early fall (March-September), although some scattered reproductive activity seemed to occur throughout the entire year. Females may have up to 3 litters per year, although 2 is more usual. Gestation was 21-22 days and litter size was 3-10, although 5-7 pups is most common. The young left the nest when 18-20 days old and were weaned several days later. Females reached sexual maturity at 6 weeks, while males matured at 12 weeks. The life span may have been as long as 6 years, had they not devoured one another in less than 3.

Note: No remnants of other animal or human victims were found, though previous census figures indicate one of the two islands was inhabited prior to the Blarina rex infestation. The information provided here is in part speculative in nature, in part based on reports found sealed on the previously-uninhabited island that detailed the life cycle of the species. Portions of these documents were water-damaged; only those detailing the life cycle and habits of Blarina rex survived. The others -- which preliminary restoration indicates may have once contained information about the origin of this peculiar and unique species -- are beyond repair.

# Director Spotlight: VINOD TALWAR

By Timothy Paxton with Chaitanya Reddy

*The horror or thriller genre in India was never as wildly popular as it has always been in the West. There were no equivalent Indian variations on the Frankenstein, Dracula, or Mummy movies during the first half of the 20th century. Prior to the 1970s horror films primarily featured men masquerading as monsters. When an actual supernatural creature did appear, the entity was typically low key or a minor element in the plot. An early example is the ape monster that popped up just in time to get put down by **TOOFANI TARZAN** (1937). When a ghost story was filmed its spiritual antagonist was always somewhat vague in haunting. There were a few rarities like the possession-themed **ZINDA LAASH** (1932, now, apparently, lost to time, and not to be confused with the 1967 Urdu "Dracula in Pakistan") and the reincarnation thriller **MAHAL** made in 1949. For the most part, there were no films that came close to presenting an actual rampaging monster routinely terrorizing folks.... they just did not exist.*

**Vinod Talwar**, circa late 1980s

The game changed with the film **DARWAZA** (1978) from the prolific Ramsay clan and Rajkumar Kohli's classic **JANNI DUSHMAN** (1979). These two film didn't deal at all with India's much loved fantasy genre: the Hindu mythology. Nor did they reflect the historical whimsy of Babubhai Mistry's **KING KONG**, (1962), or the popular Cobra Goddess sub-genre (Naag films, still popular today). Monsters in these productions didn't take a backseat to the action, they *were* the action. As much as these films were the bane of many of their day's critics, they were very popular with the masses. And their popularity was box office gold.

Director Vinod Talwar was an essential element of this early foray into the monster-tinged thrillers with his five entries dating from 1987 – 1991. Today his films have been all but been forgotten in the frenzied rush to embrace the Ramsay Dynasty and the more prolific horror directors that followed, including the sleaze masters Kanti Shah[1], Harinan Singh, and Kishan Shah who promoted more breasts than beasts in their low-budget productions.

Talwar, like some other directors in India, got a break and began his career in part because his family was already knee deep in the industry. He recalls how, one day, he was approached by his uncle. "During my college I was doing theater as writer, actor and director, when my maternal uncle, the late Mr. O. P. Ralhan, already a noted film producer and director in Indian Film Industry, came to know about my theatrical background, and asked me about my future plans."

Uncle Ralhan's company, Ralhan Productions Pvt. Ltd, was formed in 1963 and had a string of very successful hits. His important break-out film for the company was the 1966 mega hit **PHOOL AUR PATTHAR** ("Flower and the Stone") which made a super star out of its ruggedly handsome leading man Dharmendra.

Talwar says, "I told him I want to become a bigger director than you. He asked me why? I answered him: I am an actor but I know I would enjoy directing more as it would give me more control. First he stared at me and then he welcomed me on his team as an assistant director [on **PAAPI** in 1977]."

Talwar would go on to work as an assistant director for another uncle Shyam Rahlan on **SHAKKA** in 1981. Both men were known in the industry for developing popular and important films were praised for their social messages fused with emotional drama and excellent stars. While his relatives were getting all the big budgets and popular actors to work in their films,

---

[1] A prime example is the prolific director Kanti Shah who garnered a great deal of press and fan-appreciation with his 1998 action film **GUNDA**. After that hyperkinetic film's blaze faded quickly Shah, along with his buxom actress/wife Sapna, exploited the sex, action and horror genres (which will be covered in the next exciting issue of Weng's Chop). Nevertheless, there is always that proverbial shining star.

Talwar had problems securing either. "When I had a chance to direct, I had a hard time getting a good cast together. At that time the Indian film stars I wanted were not available or not allowing time in their schedules for my film. Then one day a writer, Dharamveer Ram, met me and he said, 'Why are you running after the stars why not make a suspense thriller film in which you don't require any star?' I thought over it and agreed with him. Then Ram narrated me the idea of **RAAT KE ANDHERE MEIN**. That's how I started with horror films."

## RAAT KE ANDHERE MEIN (1987)

In 1987 Talwar made his first film **RAAT KE ANDHERE MEIN** ("In The Darkness Of The Night"), a thriller with supernatural overtones and a monster, albeit all a "Scooby Doo" affair.

The film opens when a group of vagabonds kidnap a man and commandeer his vehicle, forcing him to drive to his home where they hide out from the law. There they abuse both him and his pregnant wife, killing him and leaving her emotionally scarred for years to come. Decades later the killers, who are now part of local high society, are being stalked and killed one by one by a hideously deformed monster.

At first glance you could write this film off as quickly made and cheap, except for the fact that it does feature some catchy musical numbers by Surinder Kohli as well as rapid-fire editing not common in Indian film. Talwar had a vision and knew what he wanted to accomplish with **RAAT KE ANDHERE MEIN**. The director just didn't have the time to smooth out all the bumps.

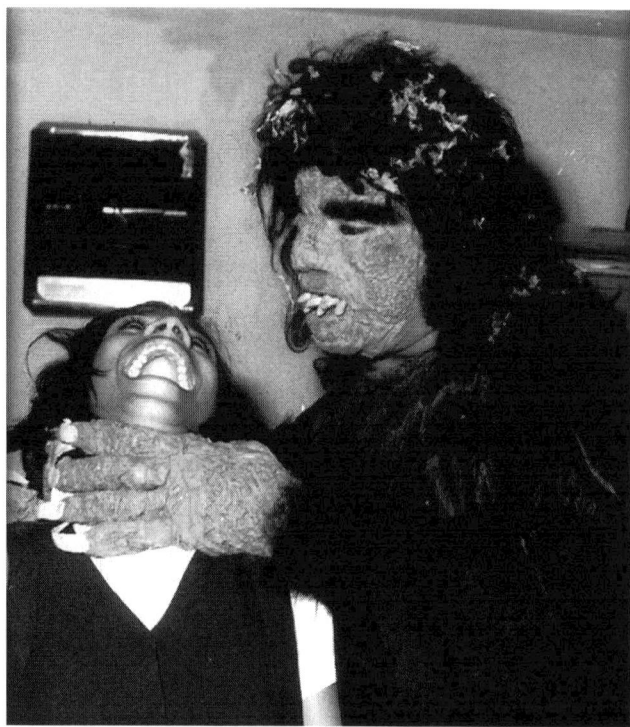

**RAAT KE ANDHERE MEIN**, rare promotional still.

It didn't help matters that the monster turned out to be a man wanting revenge for being slighted at a party. Besides a bogus monster in the plot, the director experienced an unexpected hitch when one of its stars appeared on Indian television

"My production suffered a lot during the making of **RAAT KE ANDHERE MEIN** when the film censors in India drastically cut parts of the movie," Talwar recalls. "This was mainly because my leading lady 'Deepika' was doing a mythological epic soap TV called 'Ramanyan'. She was playing the character of 'Sita' and according to Hindu religion Sita is considered a goddess. However, in my film the actress was dancing in a sexy dress. But since my posters were so attractive, and my distributors were not ready to give me more time to correct the film by doing patchwork, I released the movie as it was after the censor's cuts. But the god was with the film that, even after the continuity breaks, the film was a commercial hit. After **RAAT KE ANDHERE MEIN** people started to ask me about my next horror film project. That's how I started working on horror films."

"I would like to stress that I made **RAAT KE ANDHERE MEIN** not only for money, but to make a film where I can be recognize as a producer and director. Making this film gave me both and, more importantly, recognition."

"In the beginning when I was making **RAAT KE ANDHERE MEIN** I wasn't interested in horror movies. I enjoyed love stories and action thrillers, but during that time I started watching foreign horror films made by different directors with different special effects. Seeing those, I got more interest in horror films. My budget was limited and much of the special effects I wanted were not available in our country, so I started to work on how to direct special effect shots in my films."

Not wholly satisfied with how his first film turned out, Talwar

Left: Horror comic "Terhavi Manjil" from the 1980s; right: Pulp horror pocketbook paper back "Kaal Bhairavi" from the 1970s.

began to approach this new genre with further research, "I started to write horror stories after getting inspiration from foreign horror films[2] and reading short stories of cheap horror magazines prints in India."

Indian pulp magazines had been popular since the early 1900s. The pocket-book size publications were typically about saucy love stories, crime dramas, family and work place dramas, and horror. Sales of these paperback began to wane in the 1980s

---
[2] The classic killer kid on a tricycle scene from **THE OMEN** (1976) was borrowed for **RAAT KE ANDHERE MEIN**; the plot of the nosy neighbor kid from **NIGHT FRIGHT** (1985) was the basis for **WOHI BHAYAANAK RAT**; there is an odd killer aqua-blob scene in **KHOONI PANJA** that resembles "The Raft" segment from **CREEPSHOW 2** (1987).

due to the explosion of TV based soaps. These shows basically covered the same material as the pulps with the advantage that the TV audience did not have to know how to read. In the next decade Hindu horror comics became popular with their graphic tales of the supernatural not typically covered on the TV soaps. These publications are still popular today.

Talwar's next film was his first truly supernatural project, complete with a horrid monster and lots of frights.

## WOHI BHAYAANAK RAAT (1989)

The title translates as "That Same Horrible Night", which makes sense since this film is, for teh most part, an Indian version of Tom Holland's **FRIGHT NIGHT**.

A young couple expecting their first child is forced to stop at a shunned mansion when the birth of their child is imminent. Once inside the spooky cob-webbed mansion, the birth of their child awakens an ancient vampire who feeds on the two humans and then travels to local discos to pickup other tasty tidbits. The vampire, who can appear as a horrible monster or as a suave lady's man begins to feast on the population of the locals. That is, until one of his neighbors witnesses the monster and sets out to put a stop to this ancient horror.

Technically speaking **WOHI BHATAANAK RAAT** is clearly a finished product, that not only benefits from a better soundtrack and musical numbers by Surinder Kohli, but the make-up for the monster rivals any of the works that appeared in the films by the Ramsay.

Talwar warmly recalls, "my special make-up artist was an old man who we called Bengali Dada. He helped guide me through my filmmaking, as well as the creating the look of the monsters in my films."

Besides looking great, the monster was another first in Indian cinema. Talwar explains, "I was always thinking how could I make a different kind of film which could be a like a Western film but should feed the Indian mentality. So I mixed Western and Indian mythology in **WOHI BHAYANAK RAAT**. It was the first true vampire film in India, and the first which I show a vampire who sucks blood."

## TER TALASH MEIN (1990)

**TER TALASH MEIN** is a tale of murder and injustice... and possibly a wandering ghost story to boot. Which makes sense as the title translates into something on the lines of "In The Search For Truth". And while the film doesn't feature a horrid monster to cause mayhem, **TER TALASH MEIN** is unusual in that is it a well crafted thriller that doesn't have to rely on some hoary creature to create thrills and chills.

At this time classy horror films were under siege. Talwar explains, "while making **KHOONI PANJA** and **HATYARIN** [1990-91] I felt I should increase my budget for the films. However, the same time I was working on my films, one small budget film maker spoiled the horror film market because he was producing and selling his films for a lot less than mine. He was filling all this films with sexy scenes."[3]

---
[3] I assume that he is speaking about Kanti Shah; but professional etiquette may keep Mr. Talwar from mentioning him by name.

In the cut-throat film market in India, adding sexy scenes will boost sales. Talwar didn't want to bow to the pressure. Instead, he wanted to concentrate on making a straight-forward horror film. Butting heads with his producer caused a lot of headaches.

"At the same time that director had his films made, my distributors asked me to put sexy scenes in my films which were not linked to the story. In Hollywood they never give a reason for sexy scenes in their films, but in India you have to show the reason why you would. I didn't randomly add sexy scenes, I have a reason why my characters go through what they go through for the plot."

## KHOONI PANJA (1991)

"The Bloody Claw" was Talwar's fourth film as director and one where the monster involved is more in line with the vengeful demon that usually populates Indian horror films. The major difference, again, is that the creature stalks people both as a grotesque monster and as young woman possessed, not your typical rubber-masked villain. The Bloody Claw is a pretty cool looking monster (see our back cover for a good, full color view of this grotesque creature).

The film opens as a young couple is interrupted from an amorous evening by a girlfriend hellbent on blowing them away. Tables are quickly turned and the interloper is shot dead and her body is then deposited at a nearby graveyard for a quick and improper burial. Unfortunately the corpse has other ideas and it is reanimated by some demonic means. As luck would have it the caretaker of the charnel ground knows how to deal with supernatural entities that refuse to stay in the ground. He rushes to a nearby shrine, extracts a holy sword and brandishes it at the vengeful ghost. He forces the creature into a nearby open grave and holds it there with the mystical weapon while the lecherous couple bury the thing under holy soil... suddenly an arm pushes through the dirt to grab the leg of the woman, only to have the cursed appendage lopped off and tossed to a nearby bush. *Roll opening credits...*

What follows is a series of encounters with a gore-dripping monster that is hellbent on vengeance. Some of the scenes, including those with various tantrics performing both magic and religious rituals, are comparable to the manic Taiwanese horror films of the 80s with their magical attacks and gooey monsters.

Talwar recalls, "first I directed **RAAT KE ANDHERE MEIN** then **WOHI BHAYANAK RAAT** then **TERI TALASH MEIN**, and by that time I had watched many foreign horror films. These films grabbed my attention and helped me formulate stories that were still developing in my imagination. I then converted those ideas into Indian cinema with Indian style. If you notice all my film plots are different. At this time, while making horror films, I decided no one has shown a witch in our Indian films that's why I made **HATYARIN**."

## HATYARIN (1991)

The witch/ghost (or "Murderess" as the title translates) of a young woman is forced to kidnap and then sacrifice young brides to appease the living dead corpse of an evil trantric. In what is Talwar's most original and accomplished production, we are treated to a truly eerie movie with nary a dull moment. Talwar's trademark quick edits, crazy hand-held camera work, lovely cinematography (from the late Manish Bhatt), strong soundtrack and musical numbers (by Naresh Sharma ) and disgusting monster (Bengali Dada again, no store-bought rubber masks here!) all but enhances a story that is very Indian.

The last fifteen minutes of the film that seals the deal as our gorgeous witch pleads her case while being cornered by a good trantric, only to go full-on monster. She transforms into a bloated, fanged corpse and attacks her aggressors. Not even having her head lopped off with a magic sword can slow this beast down. Her decapitated head flicks out a deadly tongue to lash at the humans before rejoining her body so she can grow to giant-size swat and them down!

This sort of super-manic energy has never been seen in an Indian horror film (again, its sheer insanity on par with crazy Taiwanese productions). Talwar states, "to create a good thrilling ending my action director Mr. Shyam Kaushal helped me, but I always regret my producer's choice of special effect during post production. These scenes were done in my absence. I had different ideas which would have created more thrill in the entire film."

When asked if he has plans to re-release any of these films as a trilogy box set in the USA (with English subtitles): "I have sold the rights to my films **WOHI BHAYANAK RAAT** and **KHOONI PANJA**. But if there is demand I can tell rights holder to arrange their release. But regarding **HATYARIN** that film was only written and directed by me."

With the DVD release of his best work not a possibility, what about his current productions? Talwar answered, "As I mentioned earlier I stopped making horror films because there wasn't a demand for them economically. As the circumstances did not allow me to make a good horror film with a big budget, I tried my hand at an action film. The film bombed at the box office. I incurred heavy losses. Then I started working with Mr. Boney Kapoor as executive producer. As an executive producer I worked in many films with him like **SIRF TUM**, **PUKAAR**, **HUMARA DIL AAPKE PAAS HAI**, **RUN** and TV show 'Malini Iyer'. My latest film to be released was **IT'S MY LIFE**, and now we are going to start sequel of blockbuster **NO ENTRY**"

Is there hope that this unsung master of Indian monster movies will return to the genre?

Talwar's response: "Just to let you know, I am still writing plots and treatments for future horror films. I have seen many foreign horror films, and I plan to make one with a fresh approach. The film will have good scenes with good special effects, which are be cheaper in India. I am ready to make these films in the Indian language, or in any other language for that matter."

Forget what you think you've seen. Forget what you think you've heard. Neon is the new black. Just when you thought faux grindhouse would never end, along comes a crew with a passion for all things MTV-era. Their sensibilities stink of late night television, flipped collars, Members Only jackets, leg warmers and big fat lines of coke. They are the new school; creative, uncompromising and on a quest to entertain. Join Adam Brooks (of ASTRON-6) and myself as we discuss all things Astronian. Fuck the rumors, get the facts and then grab yourself a bump while you're here. Just be sure to use your own bill.

# THE INTERVIEW

# ASTRON-6: THE NU-SKOOL BRAT PACK BRINGS CELLULOID COKE

## AN INTERVIEW WITH ADAM BROOKS
### BY BRIAN HARRIS

*Brian Harris: Thanks for taking time out to answer my questions Adam! Let's talk about Astron-6, who is Astron-6 and how did you all come together to make films and shorts as a collective?*

Adam Brooks: In the early nineties the six of us met at space camp for kids. We weren't fast friends but we got along fine. they didn't have the safety precautions they have today so we were unfortunately exposed to some pretty serious gamma radiation. Fortunately though, we each developed superhuman abilities. Conor [Sweeney] was able to fly, I was good at editing etc.

Anyway, the papers were calling us The Astron Six, like we were going to be some Fantastic Four or something. But this is real life. Our powers wore off during puberty and one of the kids died of radiation exposure. There are only five of us left but we kept the name in honor of that dead kid.

*Ha! I always wanted the power of invisibility so I could sit around in the girl's locker room in high school. Turns out, I was already invisible. So when did you guys first start making shorts?*

Steve [Kostanski], Matt [Kennedy] and Conor started in high school. Jeremy [Gillespie] and I started in our twenties. There was no affordable film making when Jer and I were in high school.

*What was Astron-6's first commercial release?*

Depends how you define "commercial release." We sold a DVD compilation back in 2008 called **ASTRON-6: YEAR ONE**. Troma released a bigger compilation of our work in December, 2011 entitled **ASTRON-6**.

**FATHER'S DAY** and **MANBORG** are our first feature-length films. **MANBORG** was shot about 3 years ago now (before **FATHER'S DAY**)...but both movies premiered at Toronto After Dark 2011.

*How has the reception been for the Troma compilation, MANBORG and FATHER'S DAY?*

Better than we ever could have anticipated!

*You guys have really shot into visibility it seems, in the last two years, and I'm hearing more and more folks talking about your work. Why do you think that is? What about your styles of filmmaking differs from the usual stuff we see in genre film?*

We're making the fun, unpredictable movies that fanboys like ourselves want to see.

*I agree. With so many now jumping on the "grindhouse" bandwagon, you guys have this fucking wild 80's made-for-TV/late-night TV sensibility. Were you big fans of 80's TV and films?*

We all grew up in the 80s, visiting video stores every weekend. Back then VHS box covers and poster art mattered, and wild premises were for some reason okay.

As little kids looking at those box covers, our imaginations would run wild. The R-Rated movies were generally the most appealing but we weren't allowed to rent them, so we could only imagine all the great stuff we were missing. Now we try to make movies that live up to those fantasies.

*You've definitely succeeded. I don't think it was any surprise to fans when Troma started selling the short compilation and FD was to come out thru them. How did that all come about?*

I emailed Lloyd asking if he would do a promo for us. His assistant replied asking for money. We offered $100, then $300, but his assistant wanted $600. They eventually agreed to shoot it for us for $450. Luckily they sent the raw footage so I was able to make a good promo out of it.

A couple days after that Matt Manjourides (Troma's distribution guy) emailed asking if they could acquire our shorts. We negotiated a deal with the help of our idiot lawyer.

Soon after that Manjourides said Troma was interested in producing our first feature. (**MANBORG** was already shot at this point but took another 2 years of post-production.) Troma first offered us $5,000 to make a feature. We said, "Are you kidding?" and they replied with $6,000....again, we said "You must be joking!" and then they offered $10,000 and we stupidly said yes.

The happy ending to this story is we now have a good lawyer.

*Many people are talking about the upcoming **FATHER'S DAY** Blu/DVD release and how Astron-6 isn't at all happy about it. Is that accurate and what are you allowed (legally) to talk about concerning that release and the details behind it?*

I don't like the look of their cover art.

*Ha! It's very "video rental."*

Well compare it to the artwork Jer designed. Video rental is fine...that's our schtick...their artwork is just shitty. But, yeah, I have nothing nice to say about that company.

*This is great artwork. You're right, much better than their's. You know, the thing about Troma is is that they're too damn busy pretending to be picked on to notice that fresh young voices like Astron-6 are the only thing keeping them from fading away.*

Well I encourage the world to pick on them, and I hope to hell they fade away.

*It's a shame. Really is. The good thing is **MANBORG** is not on Troma and seems to be heating up film fests. Has it been picked up for distro and by whom?*

As I understand it, Anchor Bay will be distributing within Canada. I know Raven Banner is representing it...dunno who the foreign distributors are, or which territories picked it up, that's all Steve's business (it's his movie).

*Now, the new flick you all are working on is **BIO-COP**, right? Is that going to be a short or feature-length and what will that be about?*

It's another fake trailer. It's Steve's baby. Matt and I are in it but we shot our stuff here in Winnipeg and sent it to Steve, who shot the rest of it in Toronto. I haven't seen any of it, so I'm just as much part of the unsuspecting audience as yourself.

*Will it be going on a future compilation or will it be used to pitch the concept for a feature?*

I'm told it will be part of the **MANBORG** DVD. We also shot a lot of funny BTS interviews etc for that DVD.

*That's one I'm really looking for, I missed out on seeing it when it came to Chicago.*

*How do all five of you collaborate on ideas, scripts and the actual filming process? Is it sort of the same deal as your works on **BIO-COP** where everything is sent back and forth?*

No. It's hard. It's like any band, each project is a different combination of the five of us doing different jobs, and different percentages of the work.

*I see. Now, is your **FIREMAN** being produced for a feature-length. I read somewhere it was, if so, who will be directing?*

I have a feature length **FIREMAN** story to tell but there is no script. I tried an Indiegogo campaign but it crashed pretty hard. We're using the little bit of money that was raised to make the next two short films. I would still like to do a **FIREMAN** feature but I need money.

You didn't ask - but I will say the story is completely unlike

31

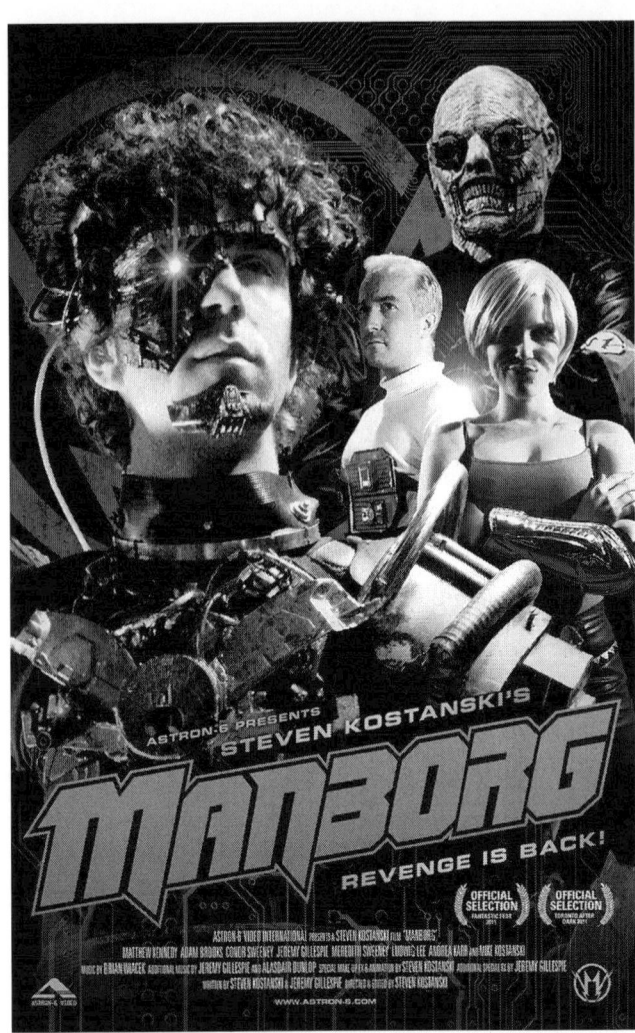

the implied story of the **FIREMAN** trailer. That is to say - the feature would not be even remotely a ripoff of **HALLOWEEN** or any typical slasher film. **FIREMAN** is as much standard slasher film as **FATHER'S DAY** is a standard revenge film. It would be directed by myself and Matt.

*Sounds like a winner! Hopefully there are some companies interested in getting your stuff off the ground. It's tiring to see some of the shit that gets budgets these days.*

*As a film fan, what have been some of the films you've enjoyed seeing in the last few years or does getting away to the theater seem to be getting harder as your projects increase?*

I liked **WANDERLUST**. I felt like they did a lot right with the new **THE AMAZING SPIDER-MAN** movie... but then they also did a lot wrong. There's not much new that gets me very excited but I'm pretty fucking excited to see **DJANGO UNCHAINED**!

*That seems to be topping everybody's lists right now. Hopefully Tarantino delivers the goods and the cult geeks can smile easier.*

*Now, FATHER'S DAY has been pushed back again, is the release out of your hands at this point? There's really nothing that can be done?*

The release has never been in our hands. I have no control, no say, and no inside info. I'll see it come out same as you.

*Basically any money Troma makes from the release will go to them or will you and the guys see any of it?*

I haven't seen any yet.

*Nothing like getting the old shaft, eh? That sucks that you guys are dealing with this shit but you all seem so goddamn creative I can't see this stopping you all from coming up with more insanity. Do you and the others have a "dream" project you'd love to tackle?*

A few, yeah, but we're not gonna kill ourselves making them for free again.

*I can see that. Man, I truly appreciate the interview, you're all busy guys so taking the time out for the zine is really cool of you. I'm sure we'll be seeing you all for years to come. Thanks Adam!*

Thanks Brian!

KEEP UP WITH THE LATEST UPDATES FROM THE GUYS OF ASTRON-6 AT

ASTRON-6.COM

ALSO BE SURE TO CHECK OUT THE DUDE DESIGNS AS WELL AT

# If Loving LAS VEGAS BLOODBATH Is Wrong, I Flat-Out Refuse To Be Right

**By Ryan Carey** (TrashFilmGuru)

*If your daughter ever brings home a guy named either David Schwartz or Ari Levin, throw the bum out of the house and lock her in the closet for the rest of her life for her own protection.*

Okay, wait just one second before you go and assume I'm on some sort of anti-Semitic tirade here. I should be clear and state that I'm referring to a couple of very specific monsieurs Schwartz and Levin here — namely, the writer-director (Schwartz) and star (Levin) of the truly unhinged 1989 shot-on-video sleazefest **LAS VEGAS BLOODBATH**. I'm sure there are lots of perfectly nice David Schwartzes and Ari Levins out there who will treat your daughter like a princess. She's free to date, or even marry, any of them — so cancel my invitation to any Neo-Nazi get-togethers you might be planning. But if she brings home a David Schwartz or an Ari Levin from Las Vegas, seriously, follow my advice — send the guy packing and never let her out of the house again.

Why would I say this about the guys behind a movie I'm going to spend the next 2,000-plus (at an early, and very conservative, guess) words at least conditionally praising, you may ask? Because, dear readers, these two fellas have some issues. And that's putting it kindly. I've spent literally decades now sifting through the absolute bottom of the horror and exploitation barrel, searching for that ever-elusive holy grail of truly wretched low-budget moviemaking, and last night, I think I just may have found it. The "perfect storm," if you will — that rare, dare I say even alchemical mixture of overwhelming technical incompetence, complete disregard for anything even remotely resembling good taste, unrestrained — nay, pathological! — misogyny, wretchedly obscene homemade gore effects, unintentionally hilarious dialogue, and offensively risible acting. I'm here to report that **LAS VEGAS BLOODBATH** has all of that in such excessive quantities that viewing it is a positively Bacchanalian experience.

Oh, sure, I'd read about this online before here and there over the years. I knew about infamous lines like "maybe he doesn't like daytime whores!!!" and "one for me, and one for this bitch!!!" — but nothing I'd read had adequately prepared me for the sheer inglorious spectacle that unfolded before my unworthy eyes last night. I figured, as far as 1980s SOV efforts went, that it couldn't top **555** for gore and tastelessness, and that it couldn't match the likes of **SPLATTER FARM** on the bad acting front. Frankly, the whole thing sounded like just a middling DIY-on-Sony-Betacam affair, and I never gave it much thought. It wasn't until I picked up the Pendulum Pictures/ Mill Creek Serial Psychos six-movie, two-DVD set (before you even ask, **LAS VEGAS BLOODBATH**, like every other flick on offer in this public-domain collection is, as you'd expect, presented full-frame, with mono sound, on a direct-from-VHS transfer with no extras whatsoever — in other words, in tried-and- true Mill Creek style, and honestly, would you have it any other way?), which I freely admit I purchased for under five bucks solely for the purpose of finally having Don Dohler's **BLOOD MASSACRE** in my home video library, and later decided, on an absolute lark, to watch some of the other shit included along with it because I was bored, that I discovered how completely and unforgivably negligent I had been in always passing up on this flabbergastingly unheralded gem of sickening, beyond-prurient, sub-gutter trash before now. David Schwartz, please forgive me. But stay away from all my female friends and acquaintances just the same.

As far as basic set-ups go, there's nothing too remarkable going on here — traveling businessman Sam Butler (Levin, who looks vaguely like the bastard offspring of a Nicolas Cage/Adrien Brody/Scott Baio threesome, if such a thing were biologically possible) comes home to Las Vegas to find his insanely big-haired, and supposedly pregnant, wife in bed with an off-duty sheriff's deputy (who looks like a moonlighting porn star — come to think of it, so does she), shoots them both dead (not that we see a bullet coming out of the gun, or even any smoke, we just hear a canned shot as Sam points the revolver in their general direction), and then goes and hits the Strip, informing no one in particular apart from the audience along the way that all

women are the same, they're all whores, they all deserve to die — you know the drill. He then comes to the conclusion, again talking out loud to nobody else, that he's going to teach a lesson to the next slut he sees walking the streets.

This being Las Vegas and all, his search doesn't take too long, and soon he's got a hooker (listed in the end credits as "The Hooker") in the car with him. He berates her for a while but she's a good sport and takes it (when a passer-by gives the two of them an ugly look and she asks "what's his problem?" we get the aforementioned "daytime whores!!!" line), and even agrees to let Sam tie her up to what I assume is some sort of outdoor power-transformer thing behind a sleazy motel in broad daylight. Sam kills her, of course, thrusting a knife up through her throat and out her mouth (again, we don't see the actual act of murder itself, but we do see the end result), then ropes her corpse to the rear of his car by the leg, drives off — and rips her leg off rather than, you know, dragging her entire dead body behind him as logic would no doubt dictate (actually logic would probably dictate that he goes nowhere at all since "The Hooker" is still tied to the electricity-meter-or-whatever-it-is, which is secured to the building).

After all that hard work, it's time for a cold one, and Sam and heads for his favorite watering hole for a beer. Not content to merely be dragging a ripped-off body part behind his car, Sam also has his (now former, if we wanna be technical about it) wife's head with him in the front seat (again, we never actually seem him decapitate her, but her mega-coiffed noggin is a constant companion to our Sin City psychopath for the rest of the flick) and brings it into the fucking bar with him! He orders two beers, we get that "one for me, and one for this bitch !!!!" line, and our guy Sam shoots the bartender in the head before he even fills the glasses. So much for that refreshment. Next, things take a really bizarre turn, even by this movie's warped standards. We're thrust, out of nowhere, into the middle of a baby shower for a pregnant member of an apparently-extant-at-the-time traveling nightclub act known as the Beautiful Ladies of Oil Wrestling (B.L.O.W, get it? Sure ya do), and the next 20-plus minutes of a barely-over-80-minute movie are spent watching, and listening to, these dull, interminably gossipy, for- the- most- part -decidedly-less-than-beautiful oil wrestlers. What do they do? What do they talk about? To be overly generous here — nothing and nothing. They have beer and donuts. They talk about how they can't wait for their pre-recorded TV appearance from New York to come on in about an hour. They play the most mind-numbingly uninteresting game of "Truth or Dare" I've ever seen. A few of them try on bikinis — including the pregnant one (yes, you read that right — and just in case you were wondering, she actually is quite pregnant, unlike Sam's wife, and yes, she's listed in the end credits as "The Pregnant Woman," even though she's referred to by her name — Barbara — several times, so even the fucking credits in this movie have a decidedly misogynistic spin to them), they talk shit about "The Pregnant Woman" when she's out of earshot (apparently she doesn't know who the father of her baby is because she fucks every guy she meets — oh, they also call her fat, one of the girls even going so far as to say "somebody needs to harpoon that whale," and evidently they all want to kick her off the team when she gets back from her maternity leave), they order a pizza, they watch themselves on TV when the show (finally!) comes on — all in all it feels like the movie's been hijacked for about 1/3 of its total run time by a promotional video for B.L.O.W — and not a very good one, at that. Most of the dialogue is quite clearly ad-libbed and it's all so hopelessly tedious that it borders, albeit quite unintentionally of course, on the sublime.

And then, bang! Just when you've more-or-less-completely forgotten about him, Sam's back in the picture. He ties the girls up and kills them one-by-one in true Richard Speck style, but Speck never had a flair for the dramatic like this! First up is "The Pregnant Woman," and honestly, they should have saved her for last, because her murder is by far the most abominably spectacular. Whatever you convince yourself Sam's not gonna do next, he does. You don't think there's any way he's going to force her to strip out of her bikini, and yet he does it. You don't think he'd possibly paw at and maul her pregnant tits, and yet he does it. You don't think the idea would even occur to him to cut her swollen stomach open, and yet he does it. You don't think he'd be twisted enough to pull the fucking fetus out of her, and yet he does it. And finally, sick and twisted as this sorry fuck so obviously is, you don't think even he would then go so far as to throw said (and now dead) fetus against the bedroom wall, and yet he does it. Friends, in the whole sordid history of on-screen slaughter and mutilation, this scene takes the cake. This is the one that can't be topped. This is the one that, blatantly unrealistic as it all is (and I guess the fact that the bedroom walls are coated with straight-from-the-ream rolls of heavy-duty paper rather telegraphs from the outset that things are gonna get pretty messy) forces you to just sit back in your chair and say to yourself "what the fuck am I watching here and why did they make it?!!" This isn't just the bottom of the barrel, this is the bottom of the bottom of the bottom of the barrel.

You'll never be the same, I promise.

How do you top that? Well, you don't, and the movie's subsequent murders, when they're even shown, are pretty tame by comparison, although the very last one merits special mention for one reason and one reason alone, and it's for this reason that I said that not just David Schwartz, but Ari Levin should be avoided like the plague by all members of the female of the species (I trust that the reasons for avoiding Schwartz are crystal-clear by now). Up to this point, Levin's pantomime-level over-the-top scenery-chewing has been, shall we say, an interesting thing to absorb. Like writer-director Schwartz, it's pretty clear he has no actual ability to perform his job (neither ever worked in the movies again after this, in case you were curious) — he just rants and raves to a quite-often-curiously-positioned camera. It's really not even fair to call what he does acting since he quite obviously can't act, which leads any rational viewer to wonder — just what the hell is he doing this for? It's damn sure not the money. It's not because he thinks it'll launch a career for himself, unless he's delusional. Could it be that he, as is apparently the case with Schwartz, whose more casual employment of downright nonchalant, off-hand misogyny (think back to "somebody needs to harpoon that whale") leads one to suspect that he's well and truly not fucking kidding when he goes OTT with it as in the cutting-open-the-pregnant-chick scene (not to mention the fact that this is the only movie I know of where two pregnant characters, one supposed and one actual, are killed — the Manson family only killed one and we're still talking about them) just plain gets off on this kind of twisted shit?

The answer, friends, is yes, and the final murder proves it. We start with Levin stripping down to his Zuba-style way-too-tight bikini briefs. Then we get the murder itself (I can't even remember how it's done). Then we have Sam setting his wife's decapitated head next to the corpse. The we have him defy all known laws of science once again by merely ripping the poor unfortunate girl's arm out of its socket. Then he licks the bloody stump-end of the arm and smears blood over his face and body. Then — moment of truth time — as Schwartz gives us a long, lingering, mid-range shot of the head on the bed, we see, off to the side, that there's a bulge in Levin's Zuba-shorts! And it ain't prosthetic effects here, people, because a) that would cost money and b) trust me, you'd make that hard-on bigger.

And that's what makes both Schwarz and Levin, and ultimately **LAS VEGAS BLOODBATH** itself, not just stupid, not just inept, not just tasteless, but downright sick. I sincerely believe that these two probably-friends are acting out some of their most twisted inner desires here. The proof is in the Zuba-briefs. I have no doubt that this movie was never "banned in over 20 countries!" as its decidedly homemade promotional poster (which makes me wonder if this thing wasn't actually screened somewhere! Oh how I wish I'd been there, but honestly I don't even remember ever seeing this on any video store shelves!), and in fact it probably hasn't even been seen in 20 countries, but these guys might just belong on the Interpol "most wanted" list regardless. The rest of the movie plays out in a fairly slapdash manner — a guy shows up at the door to help for who knows what reason and gets killed, a Jehovah's Witness shows up and Sam lobs his head off by slamming it between the door and the frame in our final physically-impossible-but-for-some-reason-not-presented-in-a-tongue-in-cheek-manner murder, and then a cop (in street clothes since there was clearly no wardrobe department, and who looks like another off-duty male porn star) breaks in and tries to save the day only to find blood, guts, and limbs spread all over the apartment, that dead fetus from a couple of scenes back lodged in the toilet, and Sam laughing his head off in a bathtub full of blood — then Sam shoots the supposed "cop," closes his eyes, opens them again, looks directly into the Sony Betacam, and the credits roll.

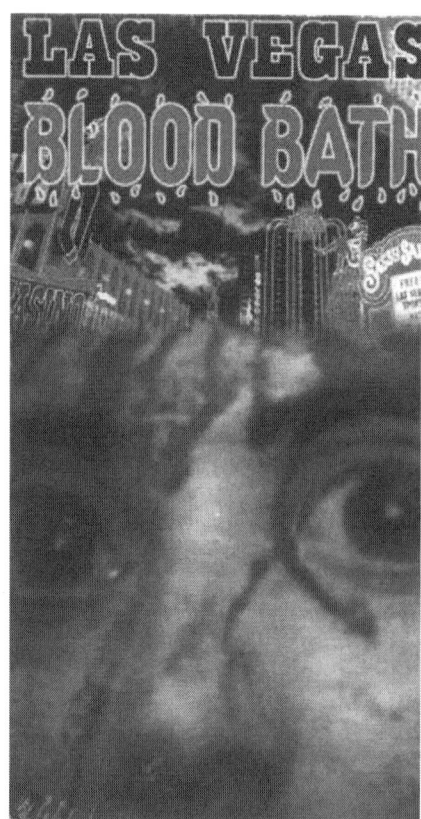

If you're not in a state of utter disbelief at this point, then you need to check your pulse — as in, to make sure you still have one. This is twisted-beyond-the-ability-of-mere-words-to-describe DIY/SOV no-budget moviemaking at its most uncompromising. What Schwartz lacks in technical ability (and that's a lot) he more than makes up for in sheer, unclean intent. While a couple of the effects guys who worked on this went on to do the same for Ted V. Mikels with **THE CORPSE GRINDERS 2** (probably more due to Mikels' proximity to the Las Vegas area than any actual skill on their part), there's nothing that is in any way even passable, much less believable, on offer here. It's so incredibly poorly paced, with such rancid dialogue and acting, and shot in such a haphazard manner, with a script that makes more or less no concessions to conventionally-accepted notions of taste, morality, or even to actual physical reality itself, that the only conceivable reason it could have been made is not because Brian Schwartz thought he could make a movie, but simply because he wanted to. And this is what he wanted to make.

And God help me, that's why I have an overwhelmingly queasy sense of admiration for this flick. The brazen temerity with which Schwartz very publicly airs his psychic dirty laundry is an amazing thing to behold. Everything about his movie is sick and wrong, and he flat-out just doesn't seem to give a fuck. With **LAS VEGAS BLOODBATH** he's delivered a genuinely psychotic opus that doesn't just push the envelope, or even rip it open — it denies its very existence and dares you to meet it, waaaaaay out here in the cold, unforgiving, wide-open expanse of its own reality, where simple rules of right and wrong, even good and evil, no longer have any meaning. It represents the outermost limit. Beyond its blood-soaked marker lies only the empty void of nothingness and unexistence. This is the last cinematic frontier.

I urge you to explore it both immediately and at your own risk.

# DR. DEATH: FROM BOY TO MAN. CULT FILM AND I

**By Gary Baxter**

My story begins way back in the early 80's, when, thanks to the home video boom, pretty much anyone with enough cash to own a VCR could take home and watch all manner of movie madness, should they be so inclined. Luckily for me my dad was so inclined, in fact he wasn't happy to just bring home the kind of films I would grow to love and eventually collect, oh no. Like many he had realized that by running two VCR's he could copy the cassettes he was hiring and by cataloging and numbering each copy he could then hire these films out to our friends and neighbors, strictly on the down-low of course! Being born in '76 meant I was pretty young when all this was happening but that didn't stop me and my brothers from seeing such gems as **ZOMBIE FLESH EATERS, NIGHTMARES IN A DAMAGED BRAIN** and **THE TEXAS CHAIN SAW MASSACRE** to name just a few! It wasn't just the horror hits we were getting to watch though, there were plenty of others to choose from, **THE EXTERMINATOR, THE WARRIORS** (we must've watched that a hundred times!), **THE NEW BARBARIANS, BRONX WARRIORS 2: ESCAPE FROM THE BRONX, A CLOCKWORK ORANGE** and more gave us plenty of action and of course there were plenty of laughs to be had with the likes of **PORKY'S, PORKY'S II: THE NEXT DAY, KING FRAT** and I recall seeing a few Terrence Hill and Bud Spencer comedies, the names of which have long escaped me. Yes indeed, I had a pretty good grounding in movies from an early age but it would be the horror genre that would stick with me the longest.

As I got older I would sit and watch Hammer movies with mum and dad, along with TV shows such as "Tales Of The Unexpected" and "The Twilight Zone" and I also got a taste of Blaxsploitation with **COTTON COMES TO HARLEM** and **SUPERFLY**, I couldn't get enough! **A NIGHTMARE ON ELM STREET** came along and really blew me away, cementing my love of fear as much as **DAWN OF THE DEAD** cemented my love of the zombie movie; I was fast becoming a fully fledged gorehound! By my mid to late teens I had begun to amass my very own VHS collection, highlights of which included **THE EVIL DEAD, STREET TRASH, HELLRAISER, CLASS OF NUKE 'EM HIGH**, both **DEMONS, BRAIN DAMAGE** and all the **NIGHTMARE ON ELM STREET** movies. My bedroom walls were awash with Freddy Krueger posters and local kids had even begun to call me Freddy due to my penchant for running round the streets in mask, hat and glove shouting things like "Hey! No running in the hallway!" in my best Freddy voice!

Then life changed, I got older, relationships came and went (as did my VHS collection) and as I became a parent I allowed

myself to be talked into letting go of my love for gore as it was no longer 'appropriate'... Hmmm, I know, big mistake...

Then it happened, now in my 30's I somehow found myself slowly getting back on the journey of discovery that'd started all those years ago and it was all thanks to a company called Shameless Screen Entertainment. Turns out they'd decided to release all three of Enzo G. Castellari's post apocalypse movies and having been a big fan of the two I'd seen and never having seen the first BRONX WARRIORS it wasn't long before I'd convinced my partner that the embossed tinned collection would be the perfect X-mas present! Well, on one of the 3 discs 20 trailers were featured, all for movies available from Shameless which really got my blood pumping, **THE NEW YORK RIPPER**? Yes Please! **TORSO**? Sold! **FLAVIA THE HERETIC**? I'll have some of that! And so began the new phase in my journey, a much more educated and calculated phase thanks of course to the internet and the well chosen titles of Shameless. But still I wanted more...

So, I was out of town on training for my previous employment when I stepped into HMV with the vague hope that someone had grown the balls to release **STREET TRASH** on DVD... and that was when I found it! A 2-disc special edition from Arrow Video, complete with poster and booklet and, yet again, info on more fine releases... **THE HOUSE BY THE CEMETERY**? Of course! MACABRE? Hell yeah! **TWO EVIL EYES**? Damn right! It wasn't long before I was snapping up Shameless and Arrow titles left and right, fast developing a taste for Giallo to match my love of straight up horror. I now own all twenty films featured in that first Shameless trailer reel as well as a few others including **CANNIBAL HOLOCAUST** and the excellent Poliziottechi classic **ALMOST HUMAN**, my Arrow Video collection has also grown to thirty-three titles including such awesomeness as **INFERNO, DEEP RED, THE BEYOND, CITY OF THE LIVING DEAD, BAY OF BLOOD** and of course the 4-disc special edition of **DAWN OF THE DEAD**! I've also managed to replace pretty much all of my old VHS collection and some of those movies I got to see as a kid back in the 80's. My reignited passion has seen my cult/exploitation movie collection grow to around 300 titles in the space of two and a half years!

Last summer I began a short run of double bills at a local bar under the name 'Dr Death's Cinema Surgery' starting with The Spaghetti Zombie Splatter Fest (**ZOMBIE CREEPING FLESH** and **THE LIVING DEAD AT MANCHESTER MORGUE**), then Masters Of The Magnificent Technique, A Grindhouse Feast From The East (**MASTER OF THE FLYING GUILLOTINE** and **SHOGUN ASSASSIN**) and then there was The Soul Brother Shakedown (**BLACK FIST** and **BLACK GESTAPO**), all good fun and something I will be looking to kick start again when the time is right.

So, that brings me to right here and now, my love of cult film has led me to writing this very article, an opportunity given me through my online association with Brian Harris, host of Creep Show Radio and I'm a month away from interviewing Darren Ward, director of the very cool gangster movie **DAY OF VIOLENCE** which is due to be released on DVD stateside real soon. I'm due to set up a Dr Death's Cinema Surgery Facebook page too, so be sure to keep an eye out and drop by and give it a *LIKE*! I hope your journey is as much fun as mine...

# The Take Away

### or, More Indian Fantastic Films that you Can Shake a Cobra At, Part 2.
### By Timothy Paxton

*I have always wondered if the movie audience the world over holds their own regional product in high regard. I can almost guarantee that they do not support their own industry as much as they do a particular brand name known since the dawn of cinematic history. One word echoes within their collective conscience: Hollywood (or "Horrywood", if you are a fan of Steven Spielberg's film **1941**). Hollywood has been the major smothering force when it comes to influencing what we, speaking as an entertainment-seeking species, want to see in our theatres, from the stars and the directors to the glamor and the hype.*

As powerful a force as Hollywood is, almost every country does have, in some form or another, their own kind industry. Since these counties are usually smaller and more isolated than the United States, there is less of a chance to share in their products. Of course, not everyone has the financial might of our bloated, self-abusive industry.

The USA, with all its talk of being democratic and open, is very, *very* xenophobic when it comes to accepting the fact that other countries have a movie industry. Heaven forbid that any country outside of the USA would produce films that we would even consider watching.

Speaking for mainstream Americans, the idea that there are films made outside of the Hollywood system is a mystery. Sure, you have those nutty Europeans making art house films, the Japanese make giant monsters movies, samurai flicks and anime, and the Chinese, well, heck they make kung fu and crazy triad/gangster films, right? Nevertheless, those of you who picked up this magazine know very well that while that statement is an oversimplification, it is pretty much true.

For as popular as American film is around the world, and as much as other countries would like to emulate its regimented approach to movie-making, the U.S. today does not make and release as many films as it used to. The sheer volume of movies released annually by independents as well as the major studios during the 1950s thru the 1970s was mind-blowing in comparison to powerhouse companies today.

Take for consideration how many films are produced in the United States in one year alone. What is the average amount? In 2011, the USA produced around 600 "professionally made" films. These are productions that had a theatrical release in one form or another. Not including direct to video or made for TV productions, there were over 1300 Indian films made in 2011[1]. A heck of a lot more films that much is for sure, although precious few of those recent productions today are as crazy as the ones I like to cover.

Almost all of the films covered in this continuing column are not readily available in the USA.

*Film cans with the night's feature film; Naaz Theatre, Mumbai, India. photo © 2009 Nain*

---
[1] Info via *chartsbin.com/view/pu4*; as a side note, after India at 1300 films Nigeria comes in second at 800 films produced in 2011, which should be disputed because most of those movies where non-traditional shot-on-video productions.

Most **do not** have English subtitles, and none are dubbed into English. Those two facts are primarily why they are not readily found for sale on Amazon (although some are available to watch on YouTube).

However, I like to buy the movies. I seriously doubt that anyone is getting residuals from my purchases, but the quality is typically higher than if I end up trying to download it from a torrent site.

By skipping four lunches a week and brown bagging it to work, I can usually save up enough money for my once a month VCD/DVD buy from indua.com, my favorite place to shop for budget entertainment. Typically I order around 20-30 titles. It may seems that I am plugging induna.com, but the fact is that they are the most consistently reliable Indian media company. Their online catalog boasts boatloads of obscure titles and they ship from Calcutta to your doorstep in three to four days. Yes, *DAYS* not weeks like some other companies better left unmentioned.

I would also like to point out that I'm going into these movies essentially blind. If the cover art looks promising, then I'm there. It's pure gut reaction. I enjoy Kant's aesthetics theory of Disinterestedness[2] and I have, in a fashion, employed that philosophy frequently throughout my life. I sit through all the titles and really, *really* pay attention to every dramatic line uttered by would-be Bollywood stars and endure all the (mostly) humdrum musical numbers. I drink this poison in on a daily basis. It's an addiction, I admit, and I take as a lot of punishment to find those few minutes of pure thrill.

I have suffered for you, and will always do so. Why? Because the following flicks are choice examples of "world cinema". The kind of celluloid monstrosities you will never find on the shelves of your local video store... outside of some select establishments in "ethnic" neighborhoods in larger cities or, I would imagine, shops in and around India.

During the "boom" of Indian horror film cinema, many of these films came in all shapes and sizes, especially during the final chaotic death throes of the late 1990s/early 2000s. All of these productions were typically based on what kind of audience they were being geared for and what kind of financing was involved. For a slight variant on this history with a twenty film sampling, you should buy (if you don't already own) Weng's Chop Issue Zero (available thru amazon.com or The Bookcase Catalog on page 52).

Let me begin with a few words of warning for you folks wishing to buy *any* of these zany films. First of all, while I am always a sucker for bombastic sleeve art on VCDs, most of what I buy does tend to fall into the category of the fantastic: horror, mythological, fantasy, weird, etc. Nevertheless, there is always

[2] If interested in Disinterestedness check out On the Origins of "Aesthetic Disinterestedness", Jerome Stolnitz, The Journal of Aesthetics and Art Criticism, Vol. 20, No. 2 (Winter, 1961), pp. 131-143, Published by:

**Inside marque; Naaz Theatre, Mumbai, India. Photo © 2009 Nain**

that rare occasion when something strikes me as unusual, be it drama, comedy (not my favorite genre), historic, mythological, or whathaveyou. Quite a few times it's the cover art of a particular film that provokes me into purchasing it. Those responsible for the sleeve art for VCDs are notorious for producing sensationalized images of stuff never seen in the film. A prime example is the art for the TNT release of Vindo Talwar's horror epic **KHOONI PANJA** (for the art check out page 25). Smack dab in the middle of the sleeve is the scaly face of Ray Harryhausen's Medusa from **THE CLASH OF THE TITANS** (1978). Her mug is boldly displayed while the visage of the actual movie monster from this production is scaled down and to the right (sadly, not as prominent as it should be as that particular monster make-up is pretty darn good considering **KHOONI PANJA** was a low-budget film). R. K. Khanna's **SHAMSHAAN** boldly reproduces the box art from The Euroshock Collection's release of Jess Franco's 1972 erotic vampire epic **EROTOKILL** (page 42). **LAASH** steals quite boldly from **GHOST STORY** (1981), and so on. The list is quite literally endless! There are even Indian horror titles that steal the artwork from other Indian films! What you see is rarely what you get.

If you are as hardcore as I am about cinema it should not bother you that these phantasmagorical films lack any subtitles whatsoever. While I have managed to pick up some bits and pieces of languages over the years, from watching other film without subtitles, the primary Indian tongues of Hindi, Telugu and Bengali are tough nuts to crack. Whereas Hong Kong films (which I watched tons of in the 80s & 90s) typically offer even crippled English subtitles, finding any of these obscure Indian films with subtitles is very rare. I believe, although don't have proof as of yet, that English subtitles for the Hong Kong film industry were mandatory by law due to that country once being part of Great Britain's Commonwealth. They exists on old HK movie prints as "burned in" images (commonly having both English and simplified Chinese characters). India shook off British rule in the 1940s, long before such a law could have taken affect. Subtitles would have helped me during some parts of these films. Seriously, if the monsters talk in these films, they chatter a lot and, like all hammy villains, love to pontificate.

Because of the sheer volume of films typically released in India, the industry itself has many levels of production quality (typically tied to assorted budgetary restrictions, etc). Many critics of "Bollywood" (as Indian Cinema is more commonly called; a misnomer as every region or state in India has its own film industry) label films Grade A thru C. Most of what I like to cover typically falls into the B and C categories, although there are the rare examples of high-profile blockbusters that are incredible films to sit through.

Babubhai Mistry's historical fantasy film **KING KONG** is one such borderline production.

## KING KONG
(1962, D: Babubhai Mistry, *VCD, no subtitles*)

Despite its title, this film doesn't refer to a giant marauding ape, but rather to a popular Hungarian born pro-wrester of the era. Born Emile Czaja, his stage name of King Kong pretty much matched his huge (some would say fat) stature. King Kong retired in the late 50s and turned to acting in films. This was also the first film of Dara Singh, another hugely popular grappler turned actor. It was this film that won him the hearts of millions of adoring fans guaranteeing him roles in many future production playing the likes of monkey god Hanuman, handsome princes, etc. Singh would later turn to directing and producing.

The film opens with the arrival of Singh, on the scene of a giant monster attack. Yes, a *giant* monster in an early 60s Indian film. A very rare instance indeed! This four-legged creature bellows smoke and is in the process of terrorizing a beautiful maiden when the burly ex-wrestler does his rescuing bit. Singh lets the monster pick him up in its slavering jaws so he can jab a spear down its gullet. Once the monster is dispatched our tale of dueling wrestlers can commence.

The late Babubhai Mistry, 2010 at his home with props and memories from from when he was one of India's bigggest directors.

photo © Shashwat DC

**KING KONG** is quite possibly the best of the this sub-genre of the mythologicals/fantasy if you take into consideration the adherence to continuity in plot, production and musical numbers. The monster is fairy impressive, and this is coming from what was usually a poverty-ridden Indian film industry. Special effects wasn't usually a film's point. Most Indian films were more concerned with where to drop in the music, rather than how terrifying the minster looked on screen.

It is pretty obvious that the creature effect for this film is two men in a fancy-looking horse costume. As silly as you may think the thing is, the beast is a kissing-cousin to an assorted denizens from around the cinematic globe: from the obvious men-in-suits of the Japanese giants to the puppets from Italy's **GOLIATH AND THE DRAGON** (1960, D: Vittorio Cottafavi) and the USA's **THE MAGIC SWORD** (1962, D: Bert I. Gordon).

The comparison to the American special effects creator and director Bert I. Gordon is not that far off the track as director Babubhai Mistry (who passed away in 2011 at the age of 90) had also been a pioneer in Indian fantasy films since the mid 1930s. In a 2008 interview with ShashwatDC[3], Mistry recalls how he got his start in the business. While working as a custom designer on a film, he was approached by a producer, who had just come away from a Bombay theatre that was showing James Whale's **INVISIBLE MAN**. Mistry was asked to come up with some effects work on a new film. He contributed "trick effects", as they were called back then, for what turned into the 1936 Indian "Invisible Man" film **KHWAAB KI DUNIYA** ("Dreamland").

Known as the father of 'trick scene directors', Mistry was the effects master, and sometimes director, of over 300 films and TV productions. His work included many mythological and devotional films, those films which, due to their inherent fantastic nature, begged for very special effects. These films told the varied fantastic myths of the Hindu God and Goddesses, and include **PAWAN PUTRA HANUMAN, MAHABALI HANUMAN, SAMPOORNA RAMAYANA,** and **NAAG PANCHAMI**; fantasy films like **KING KONG, HATIM TAI, MAGIC CARPET,** and **SATI NAAG KANYA**; and thriller/fantastic films such as **NAGLOK**. Sadly, the master trickster was forced into retirement when a new era of high-tech effects work by a younger generation caught the attention of producers. His last film was the 1991 cobra goddess devotional drama **MAHAMAYEE**.

Not all producers relied on their studio's 'trick scene directors' to add excitement to their plots, some just lifted a whole special effects sequence from other films. The 70's caveman epic **AADI YUG** is a prime example of this blatant act of plagiarism.

## AADI YUG
(1978, D: Prasad; *VCD, no subtitles*)
...And speaking of giant Japanese monsters, **AADI YUG** might be as close as you will ever get to a legit *kaiju* film even though the producers of the film didn't drop a dime, nickle or penny to deliver the thrills. **AADI YUG** is a film about the beginning of humankind. To hammer the point home, the opening credit sequence has a slide show our evolution from monkeys to humans by way of a series of illustrations that looked as if they were lifted from an array of magazines and books.

The film opens with a cosmic explosion as our world is created and a naked man is laying in the dirt near an ocean's edge. Our protohuman shakes off the after affect of his auspicious birth and gets to his feet in time to see an equally naked woman in a boat off shore. He rescues her and they romp about their new world hand in hand and then get down to business.

Later, when the kids start popping up, our original human must point out that there are dangers in the world. This is where the big "oh no they didn't" moment occurs for Godzilla and Toho studio fans. This next scene must have been cobbled together to keep the creationists happy as a "caveman" battling a "dinosaur" is tossed into the mix. The big monster scene in **AADI YUG** turns out to be the final six minutes from Inshio Honda's 1965 classic **FRANKENSTEIN CONQUERS THE WORD**. Frankenstein is seen slugging it out with the giant monster Baragon until the that films' blazing end. Whoever lifted this sequence didn't even bother keeping both films within their original aspect ratio. **AADI YUG** was lensed in 4:3 (as were a lot of films from this time) while the 16:9 footage from Honda's film was squashed down to fit, rather than using a pan and scan source.

After losing one of his sons to Baragon, our saddened father turns away from the scene of carnage. His family then encounters the proverbial man-in-an-ape as the hairy humanoid grabs one of the ladies of the tribe and runs off with her. That monster is quickly subdued by the men and tossed into a river. Oh, the exciting times we had back then in the dawn of history! The film drags on a little bit longer then ends rather ambiguously.

**AADI YUG** was release around the same year as another Asian "origin story" film from Taiwan called **IN THE BEGINNING** (1979, D: Shan Lo), but lacked the latter's gods vs giant monsters storyline. Rather, director Prasad opted for stealing the scene from Honda's film rather than ponying up the cash for his own rubber-suited monster. Which is too bad, as it could have made the film more interesting than it was. The same could be said of the rather crude censorship because of the (rare) frontal nudity, thanks to the frolicking Adam and Eve from the beginning of the film. Shabby paper cutout of rocks, trees, and not sure what else were inserted post-production making for some oddly arty sequences. A word of warning: there is no dialog in this film, and there are NO musical numbers, making **AADI YUG** a real testament of endurance.

---
[3] shashwatdc.com/2011/08/babubhai_mistry/

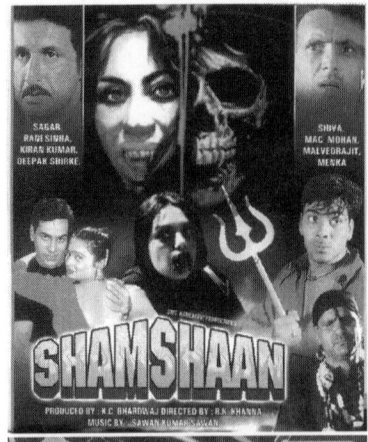

*At this point the classical sense of fantastic absurdity takes a back seat to cheaply made horror films. I subscribe to the theory that many crappy no-budget films trump their bloated siblings with enthusiasm over finances. Not all of them are in the same category of The Ramsay's horror films or those by the lesser appreciated filmography of Vindo Talwar (see page 22). These films are typically made outside the system. These are truly indie productions, and most rely on the titillating antics of scantily clad leading ladies and special effects men mugging the camera in store-bought rubber monster masks.*

*The following films are by no means the only supernatural-cum-horror films produced in India at the time. There are better known ones, which I many cover in a future issue of Weng's Chop. B Vijay's 1981 film MANGALSUTRA is a crazy EXORCIST inspired horror film. Santram Varma's KRISHNA COTTAGE (2004) and the early films by Ram Gopal Varma are worth checking out. There are also weird art-house titles such as Aparna Sen's 1989 SATI (a sobering example of magical-realism), and Vikas Desai & Aruna Raje's lovely low-key supernatural thriller GEHRAYEE (1980).*

## SANSANI
(1981, D: Irshad; *VCD, no subtitles*) "The Sensation"
An early film that wants to be a thriller, but lacks any real cohesive plot to produce any. A hooded killer is on the loose in this Indian *giallo* movie. This is another example of a humdrum flick that sported sleeve art that was way more entertaining than the actual film. As far as Indian low-budget thrillers go the film *looks* good and has some entertaining musical numbers that aren't just randomly dumped into the film's running time. The soundtrack is scored by Hemant Bhosle, although **SANSANI** doesn't appear on any official list of works. Still, a viewer can't help but feel that this film could have been better if given half the chance. A white-sari clad ghost haunts the lives of two men who disembark a train in a small town. Murders and spookiness are afoot, but it is all a farce as the female apparition turns out to be part of convoluted revenge scheme.

## SHAITANI AATMA
(1998, D: Harinam Singh; *VCD, no subtitles*)
Director Singh is one of "those" directors who seemingly sets up his camera and ambles away (going for a smoke possibly) and letting what happens happen. The few critics that cynically praise his work call **SHAITANI AATMA** an example of "Outsider Cinema". Whatever you want to say about the film, this is quite possibly the best of the batch due to the WTF factor.

Prolific actor, producer and director Harinam Singh, who would go on to make the equally absurd **SHAITANI DRACULA** in 2006 (see Weng's Chop #0) with pretty much the same cast and crew, has thrown down another silly romp thru plastic fangs, store-bought rubber masks, and bouncing babes. A group of women (including Sonia Thakur and Shweta Fule, the true highlights of this production) dance and jiggle throughout the grounds of a haunted mansion stalked by a pathetic monster. After some truly atrocious dance numbers resembling slumber parties only slightly out of control, the supernatural entity is beaten up by some manly men and then stabbed with Shiva's trident (the ever-trusty weapon of choice in these films). **SHAITANI AATMA** is a slack-jawed production that is mindlessly entertaining at best and mind-numbingly laborious at worst. I enjoyed it immensely.

As abusive as Singh is, spoon-feeding us this insanity, at least his product was entertaining. Our next film is R. K. Khanna's **SHAMSHAAN,** and it is just plain *bad*.

## SHAMSHAAN
(2000, D: R. K. Khanna; *VCD, no subtitles*)
A young woman is raped and left for dead by a gang of thugs. She returns from her shallow grave a deranged "ghost" and kills her abusers one by one, going as far as to dress up as a wormy, boil covered nightmare just to dispatch one of the men. Later she is caught by gang and thoroughly knifed to death. Her boyfriend picks up where she left off, until, after stabbing and killing the last rapist by running him through with a trident, he is arrested by the police. The End. Typically, crappy films like this one have at least one entertaining musical number, even if its choreography is beyond hope. Nope, they're as dull and sad as the rest of the film.

## DANGEROUS NIGHT
(2003, D: Muneer Khan, *VCD, no subtitles*)
You would think that the Scooby Doo element of the killer in a monster ape suit would have started to wear pretty thin by 2003. Nevertheless, the hairy gorilla monster that's killing off folks in this potboiler turns out to be a human and he then goes to trial for the last half an hour of this dreary mess. (See what I have to put up with just to make sure you don't waste your hard earned dollar and two hours.)

Dreadful masked monsters, sad musical numbers, and poor direction had me almost comatose. The only saving grace is the appearance of Sapna Tanveer as one of the bosomy ladies in distress.

*A very pleasant surprise greeted my tired brain with the next VCD.*

## ZAKHMI NAAGIN
(2004, D: Suresh Jain, *VCD, no subtitles*)
Just when all hope seemed lost and my world was going to close up around me I popped in the first VCD of **ZAKHMI NAAGIN** and I was saved. First, let me clue you in on a little secret: while I can sit through just about anything no matter how horrible, there are times when I fast forward or skip sequences altogether. However, I will ALWAYS watch a Nagin film just to see how sexy the cobra lady will be. **ZAKHMI NAAGIN** was a very pleasant surprise after the last few major disappointments.

A big city film crew is sent to a rural hotel to do a sexy photo shoot. The group piles into a company jeep and they head off to a remote village. The village is in the middle of celebrating Nagapanchami, an important snake-worshiping holiday for most of India[4]. At this point in the film we are introduced to the Naagin, a snake goddess who is super hot as she shimmies through the first musical number. She cavorts through a traditional Nagini dance with her equally good-looking male snake companion. Sadly, at the end of their sexy song, when both naagin revert to their snake form and slither across a dirt road, the male deity is run over by a jeep and killed. The she-snake is horrified to find that her mate has been squashed by careless driving on the part of our film crew. She swears vengeance and thus begins the tale.

Since **ZAKHMI NAAGIN** is primarily an A Certificate (adult), Grade C dry-hump sex film with some horror thrown into the plot, there is an ample (and I mean *AMPLE*) amount of heaving bosom popping out of practically every scene.[5] Most Indian sexy films do not feature full or even partial nudity. Director Suresh Jain probably did get a rise out the audience with a few quick scenes of passionate full-on kissing, which is a no-no by Indian standards[6]. The titillating titular creature woos various men with her body, leading them on by their gonads until she has them alone. She then coolly dispatches them.

The other ladies in the film have their own lustful moments during two dance sequences. In one such number two couples are getting into the mood and another woman is prancing in underwear for one of the photographers. She suggestively attempts to fellatio a lit candle without singeing her eyelashes or brows.

In the end our cobra lady is outsmarted by the remaining humans and she too is run over by same jeep that killed her mate. The film ends as the two creatures are reunited in the afterlife. Had the production budget been more substantial then this film could have been even better. As it turned out the funds were probably spent on booze and hookers, rounding out the production with mostly cheap synth based musical numbers, documentary footage of Nagapanchami ceremonies, so-so acting, and limited special effects. Nevertheless, the major jiggle factor of actress Tanveer did help make this an excellent VCD buy at 95¢.

## THE BUDGET DVD SET...
As crummy as most of these films are with their lame monsters, I have come to appreciate them for what they are: examples of almost pure cinema. There is a popular catch-all term that is bandied about by critics called "Outsider" cinema. This oft-coined term comes from the equally popular Outsider art scene involving artists that create without any formal training whatsoever. Similar to the Art brut and naivete "folk" scene that triggered excitement in the art world in the early 1960s and 70s (an art movement whose linage can be traced back to the insane asylum art that had begun to be collected in the 1920s and 30s). For all intents and purposes, these films could very well fit right into that movement.

You could also approach them on a totally different level; that

---

[4] This is typically in celebration of Lord Krishna's domination over the river snake demon Kaliya Naag, and involves folks putting out milk for snakes to drink, as well as making snake art and snake music.

[5] For those of you panting to see more of the actress in this film, there MAY be a reel of nude scenes floating around sitting in a warehouse in India. A good many of these Adult Features where released without certificates in softcore variants which played in sleazy movie houses all across rural India. A few of these edits have made it onto DVD as it evident by Kanti Shah's 2003 **PYAASA HAIWAN** which I reviewed in Weng's Chop #0.

[6] Kissing or any public form of passionate affection is not the social norm in most parts of India, although due to the worldly education of the current generation what we westerners would consider normal is now slowly becoming acceptable... if not begrudging so.

of an alternate reality. In this realm of existence, the world is populated by scandalously clad young women are being stalked by lecherous sex-crazed men as well as supernatural creatures. These entities enter our reality in a form which we could relate to from everyday experience. And what is more mundane than a cheap rubber Halloween costumes. It is the closest that we have to understanding their nature of being.

Okay, that's a little far-fetched, but considering that no one has ever seen a demon or alien or such monster, then some thing could very well look like a crappy trick-or-treater. Or maybe Hello Kitty.

Earlier films like the werewolf movie **JANNI DUSHMAN** (1979) and **MANGALSUTRA** (1981), with its spiritual possession theme, were essentially made for wider audience appeal, although their distribution was severely hampered by censorship and outright bans. Other horror films were part of this movement in the late 70s and early 80s, echoing the non-traditional influential western terrors, albeit spiced with Indian flavor. These were expensive endeavors that took too long to make and didn't play well in some of the seedier theatres. The exploitation of the sleaze-hungry lower-class was just around the corner and the popular horror sex mash-ups of the 90s that were brewing were ready to be served.

"Six-In-2-Super-DVDs" packs are fairly common now, and can be a better method for collecting a vast catalog of films without exerting too much energy. For the most part companies tend to have genre-based anthologies covering horror, sexy, action, mythological, drama, historical, comedy and so on.

Buying one or more of these collections may be ideal for those of you who don't like VCDs (which are notoriously buggy). Companies, like Moser Baer Entertainment (one of India's largest producers of home video), do offer DVD collections of the more obscure titles. As popular as this format is, the visual quality suffers immensely. Imagine cramming three 120 to 160 minutes movies on one single-layer disc. That's a lot of compression and digital artifacts pop up frequently. Six films for $2.50 is a bargain even if their transfers don't merit that "Super DVD" moniker that the sleeve art promises. Their source material is pretty much the same as the VCDs... some are even are widescreen if that matters to you. For those of you wondering, these are thread-bare DVDs with no bonus material whatsoever – no trailers, no subtitles, no documentaries or commentary. Just the movies.

## DISK One: *THE B-GRADE*
*This set splits their films rather neatly divides the good from the bad. Disc 1 features older and much better productions. Or at least these films that tried to be something more than your usual mundane monster and raunchy risqué gobbledygook.*

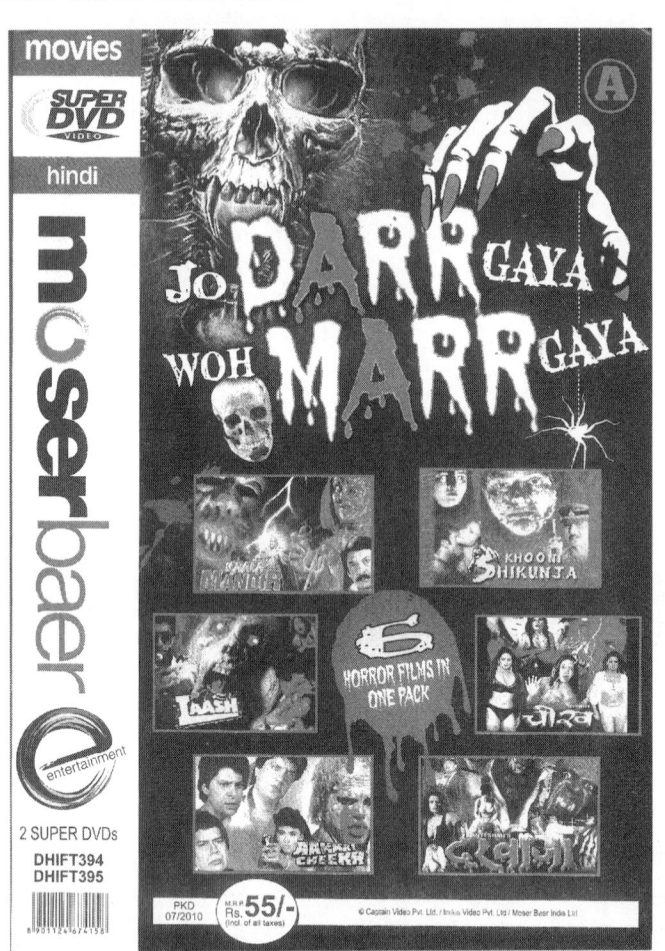

### AAKHRI CHEEKH
(1991, D: Kiran Ramsay, *DVD no subtitles*) "The Final Scream". Of all the films covered so far this has the most polish. Of course, it also has the biggest horror/thriller genre production company behind it. For those who aren't familiar with the Ramsay name, this cinematic dynasty is pretty much the reason for all of these horror films. If you're interested in the entire catalogue of and the story behind The Ramsays and the incredible hold they had on the "horror creature" genre, search out and read "Ramsay International" by Rishi Majumder originally published in May 2012 issue of *Motherland Magazine*.[7]

An evil master of the dark arts transforms into a hideous slobbering monster and kills off assorted women. Eventually he is caught by the police and executed... however, as with many films of this ilk, the monster is not truly destroyed. The evil is able to reincarnate and possess anyone within the immediate vicinity, and in the process they are transformed into the hulking creature. It's up to two yogis to discover the creature's unholy source of power and destroy it.

As Ramsay films go, **AAKHRI CHEEKH** is average. Kiran's direction lacks the punch and polish of earlier horror films by his brothers Shyam and Tulsi; their best being **BANDH DARWAZA** (1990), **TAHKHANA** (1986), and **DARWAZA** (1978). Just to keep things moving there are a few entertaining musical numbers by Bappi Lahiri, a popular person to score your films as he's written over 400 to date.

### LAASH
(1998, D: K. Mansukhal, *DVD no subtitles*)
Not to be confused **ZINDA LAASH**, which is an older and much better Pakistani horror film from 1967 (aka **DRACULA IN PAKISTAN**). A popular theme with a great many horror films is the "murdered woman returning as a vengeful demon" plot. The film opens up with a wonderfully eerie opening credits track by Usha Khanna. The ghost of a woman murdered by a

---
[7] , issue #7 "Ghost Stories".

high-stakes gambler returns from the dead to kill men who abuse her gender. She possesses the bodies of the woman being defiled, who then turns into a hideous (rubber-mask wearing) monster. The creature mortally wounds the lecherous man then transforms into the lovely likeness of our dead vigilante, where upon she flips a playing card on his dying body. She leaves the body of the now totally confused and horrified woman who was attacked. Eventually she tracks down her killer and polishes him off, returning back to the land of the dead where she hopes to find peace.

**LAASH** could have been a whole heck of a lot better if it wasn't for that cheap costume department. You know, the guy who was given five bucks to go to the Indian Wal-Mart and buy an ill-fitting rubber monster mask. As for the ghoul featured on both the film's poster and the VCD sleeve art, yep, it is nowhere in the movie. The grotesque corpse is the work of master special make-up artist Dick Smith from the 1981 film **GHOST STORY**.

## KAALA MANDIR
(2000, D: Hemant-Kamal, *DVD no subtitles*).
The film's credits slam us with a promising rag-tag instrumental genre-stretching disco number and a lengthy monologue explaining the plot of the film. W are introduced, one by one, the principle players in this horror film. This odd introduction almost has me wondering if this film is a sequel to another thriller. A large black stone statue of the goddess Kali in full-on vengeance mode is on display in a snake infested temple, setting the mood for what is to follow.

A young woman becomes entangled in what seems to be a high-stakes escort service as a result of a run-in with the Madame running the business. The Madame has some of her goons rape and attempt to murder the woman by bashing her head in with a rock. Mortally wounded she staggers into a temple ruin dedicated to Kali where she collapses dying at the base of the statue. The grizzled form of the temple's priest asks that his goddess do something, and the dead woman is reanimated. Alternating between the likeness of a beautiful woman and a rotting corpse she proceeds to dispatch her murders one by one.

Yes, this sounds pretty much like the same plot of a lot of these Indian horror films, however, the monster design is better than usual (a bloated corpse in rags). Fearing for her life the Madame flees to the old ruins and pleads with Kali to save her from the apparition. Kali turns a deaf ear to the cries of the woman as the demon smashes her head in with a large stone. Sounds silly, but this film delivers the goods in both creature thrills, action, and a decent synth-heavy "background" score by Priyesh Vakil who is now a famous composer (he had worked with the famous Music Director duo of Laxmikant-Pyarelal).

## *DISK Two: THE C-GRADE*
*The lack of a budget hadn't affected the look of horror films prior to 2000, when some of the earliest of Kanti Shah's horror film were being made (Shah had been involved with cheap action and "jungle" film since 1988; more on that next issue). In comparison, the earlier works by The House of Ramsay from the 80s thru the 90s which seemed stylish in their execution. Their costumes, sets, and meager trick photography managed to be somewhat effective. Shah and the gang were, for the most part, lackadaisical in their execution of any script (the existence of a script may be called into question) Most of their plots involved the four chintzy basic food groups: Spooky mansions or hotels, rubber-faced creatures or traditional white funeral clothed spirits, sexy ladies and horny guys (and/or monsters), and trashy dance numbers. Toss in a good measure of running around screaming (and that ever-present and annoying stock footage of lighting and thunder) and you have a movie made by this close-knit group of filmmakers.*

## KHOONI SHIKUNJA
(2000, D: Yesheantt, *DVD, no subtitles*)
**KHOONI SHIKUNJA** is a quickly made horror film starring some very familiar faces, including that of Anil Dhawan, a very popular actor in all sorts of films (including **LAASH** and **AAKHRI CHEEKH**). This time around we are treated to yet

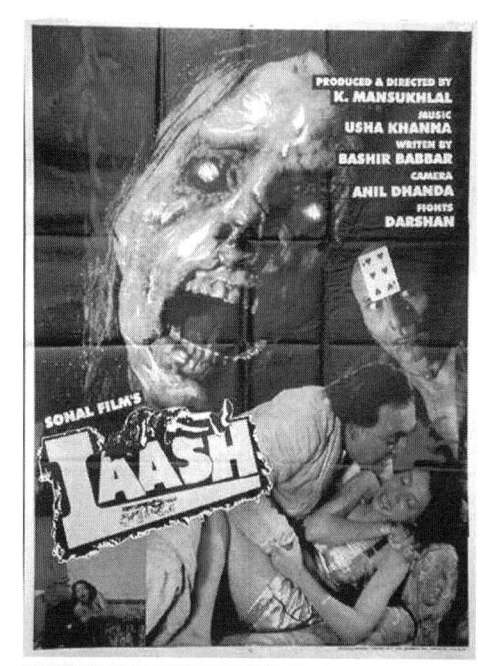

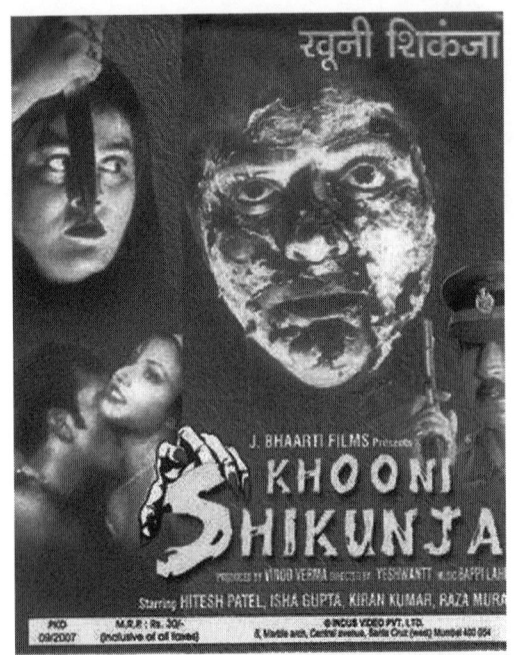

another one of those pesky, vengeful she-demons that stalks and slaughters the men who raped and killed her. She appears as a frightful boil-covered specter oozing blood and rage, either personally attacking an individual or possessing the body of a young woman to carry out the deed.

But just when you think you've seen this film before, there's an oddball plot twist. It seems that there is more to the plot when it becomes clear that some money-hungry humans are behind the creation of the demon, and they posses a way of controlling it for their own nefarious needs. The ghost-possessed young woman picks off the family members of a rich household as well as the men who raped and killed her. In one absurdly bizarre scene she turns into a baby doll that attacks and bites one of her rapists.

The film draws to a close as the demon, who has been possessing the body of a young man's girlfriend, turns on those who created her. It is destroyed when the god Shiva intervenes. Oh wait, the film doesn't end at the destruction of the demon. To flesh out the running time to to almost two hours, there's a six minute fight sequence complete with comedic bumbling, heroic fisticuffs, and a cat fight. Silly stuff.

*This is as good place as any to mention that the Indian film industry produces multi-genre films as a rule. Most of you are very aware of the musical numbers that pop up at seemingly random moments in most (but not all) Indian films. These toe-tapping splashes of color, dance and song are usually an alternate narrative to what can be typically a very plot-heavy film. Bollywood film music is called filmi music, which means "of films" in Hindi.[8] These moments of frenetic nuttiness add to the film's overall surreal appeal. But the comedy bits that pop up out of nowhere can be soul-crushing stretches of dreadful tomfoolery. Whereas filmi carries the narrative, the slapstick actions of "funny looking" actors mugging for the camera or pulling faces put a stop to any of the forward movement achieved in all of Indian cinema in general. In the horror and drama genre this can be devastating.*

*Almost every Indian film has these comedic episodes. As one director told me, "Here in India we makes films that are typically 150 minute long. Indian cine goers get headaches after watching continuous horror scenes, so we insert comedy scenes as a way to balance out the scary parts. These scenes are there to relax to audience". It's a formula that works for them, but makes me cringe.*

Each of the following films are examples of this mood-killing nonsense.

## DARWAZA
(2002, D: Kanti Shah, *DVD no subtitles*)
"The Door" is a film that is smack dab in the middle of director Kanti Shah's current filmography. Kanti began his career in the late 90s with a handful of low-budget but very popular drama/action flicks including the much ballyhooed **GUNDA**. Kanti specializes in sleazy Adult features relying heavily on heaving bosoms in wet saris and cheaply made thrills. As with many other directors he relies on a stable of actors and actresses who routinely appear in all of his films. In turn they supply him with the perfunctory crap acting that is core to every Kanti Shah production.

**DARWAZA** (not to be confused with the earlier 1978 Ramsay film) stars Shah regulars Arun Mathur, Anil Nagrath, Amit Pachori, Sapna, and Vinod Tripathi who are all involved in a yet another take on the monster in a haunted mansion. A young woman (the shapely Sapna, Shah's wife) is terrorized by the ghost of a sexual psychopath. Can the tantric master in a bad bald wig save her from the demon's clutches? Yes... but not before Sapna gets a lot of screen time in various forms of undress. Even the usually very entertaining but awful scores by Sawan Kumar Sawan are pretty weak. Each musical number looks and sounds like a rehearsal.

---
8 en.wikipedia.org/wiki/Bollywood#Bollywood_song_and_dance

**DWARZWA** could have been a fun time, but suffers from some truly awful cinematography and editing. Entire scenes and cut-aways are so out of focus as to leave you blurry eyed from trying to make sense of the visuals. Unlike Spanish director Jess Franco, who is known for his use of lingering soft-focus abstractions, Shah appears to be technically inept or just apathetic. It's not as if he can't make a competent film... he can. Whereas Franco has a vision (spacey and transcendental as it is) Shah suffers from sheer laziness.

## CHEEKH
(D: Kanti Shah, *2004, DVD no subtitles*).
Here's a rarity in Shah's filmography: a film that is pure delightful trash. Sexy thrills and inept horror arises when a ghost possesses young women and sends them on hell-bent missions to kill dastardly men. Basically, like most other films by Shah, this is an excuse to have gorgeous young women like actress "Sapna" dance around in lacy underwear or take long showers in skimpy bathing suits to very awful musical numbers (which may not be such a bad thing). Soon The demon is cornered by brave local police officers and, with the help of a Catholic priest, she is exorcised. Happily this film is only about the possessed Sapna, who struts around in revealing garments when killing men. The only rubber-faced monster typically found in a Shah production happens to be her boyfriend getting frisky with some role playing. The very fact that there are no cheap monsters in this film, but instead voluptuous ladies possessed by a ghost, makes this Shah's most accomplished work in this much abused genre.

The film stars the late Rami Reddy as the devout Catholic priest that assists in snuffing out the pesky ghost. This was an odd role for this very imposing South Indian actor who was typically typecast as a villain, an evil tantric (as in the 1995 Telugu Durga goddess film **AMMORU**) or the leering rapist or henchman (see just about every other film he's been in).

Shah's **CHEEKH** should not be confused with the 1985 film by the same name by Mohan Bhakri (who made the pretty cool horror films **KHOONI MAHAL** and **KHOONI MURDAA**) or the 1991 Ramsay production **AAKHRI CHEEKH**. Rest assured that once you've seen this film, you couldn't mistake it for one made by anyone else.

## *FINAL THOUGHTS...*

As for the future of Indian horror and monster films, that's pretty much up in the air. Despite what you may think after reading this article, I've only concentrated on a tiny fragment of the horror genre. Not all of the horror films from the period covered were crummy little productions. Some, like Kiran Ramsay's **AAKHRI CHEEKH**, are the cream of the crop during this time.

I deliberately left out all but one of the Ramsay horror films, as they have been extensively analyzed and reviewed by other authors. My concentration will almost always be on the lesser known and least appreciated productions.

These films were made for an audience of "Jhuggie-Jhopdi", as coined by the late actor/director Joginder Shelly in a 2004 interview with the online newspaper *The Hindi*. The term means "slum" or "the lower class", and refers to the usually raucous folks that attend films made by him, and his buddies Kanti Shah, Kishan Shah, Ramesh Lakhiani, Harinam Singh, and Saleem Suma.

There are some directors that make their films with anyone available, and then there are those who have a set of core actors. There are also those directors that have a muse to inspire them to produce film after film. Spanish director Jess Franco had Howard Vernon and Lina Romay, Ingar Bergman had Max von Sydow and Liv Ullman, Tim Burton has Johnny Depp, and there's Quentin Tarantino witjh Uma Thurman. These are people with whom the director has or had a special bond. Indian director Kanti Shah's muse is his voluptuous wife Sapna Tanveer aka "Sapna" as she is better known in most of her films.

Sapna's career began when, in 2000, she bounced into low-budget Indian cinema in the film JALLAD NO.1 for Shah. Since that fateful debut she has appeared in over 30 films that I aware exist. Her characters typically require her to partially disrobe in some fashion, get soaking wet in a form-fitting sari, prance around in a bikini or, for some of her best roles, Sapna is decked out in leather when she's a tough as nails babe who is usually armed to the teeth.

A short list of some of her films includes those from a wide range of genres including horror, action, comedy, and drama (well, sexy drama): **PYAASA HAIWAN, ZAKHMI SHERNI, BEDROOM, PYAASI BHOOTNI, PYAASI NAGIN, KHOONI, ILAAKA, MAUT, BHOOT KA DARR, QATIL CHUDAIL, EK RAAT SHAITAN KE SAATH, SAR KATI LAASH, MAUT KE PECHHE MAUT, PYAASI, VIRANA, CHEEKH, DARWAZA**, and **FREE ENTRY**. She has worked with other directors other than her husband, but she's Shah's special go-to actress when sex is needed to spice up one of his pot-boilers.

More on the films of Sapna and Kanti Shah in forthcoming issue of Weng's Chop. DON'T MISS IT!

The rise of the internet and easy access to digital media has made it easier to disseminate American and other Western genre films. Big studio, as well as independently produced genre films, have become increasingly influential in Indian cinema. As a result the kind of low-budget films like those I just reviewed have all but vanished.

Back in the bygone era of the 70s and 80s it was usually the directors of films like **JANNI DUSHMAN** and **BANDH DARWAZA** that saw western flicks and decided to incorporate them into their lexicon. During the 90s into the turn of the century video media gave widespread exposure of additional Western films to hungry Indian film goers. To meet these needs directors like Kanti Shah churned out sleazy sexy horror film assembled so cheaply and quickly that it would have made Takashi Miike blush. This ramped up production ran thru the mid 2000s, only to fade as quickly as it arrived.

I have mixed feeling about some of the more recent example of "Bollywood" horror. The sleaze factor is still abundantly apparent when you consider that, again, the internet has a lot to do with pushing the moral envelope in India. This is a country that is steeped in sexual puissance since antiquity. The much ballyhooed Karma Sutra comes to mind, as does the Khajuraho Group of Monuments temple complex of Khajuraho, Madhya Pradesh with its sexually explicit carvings and statues. Boobs and rampant sexual pleasure are everywhere in Indian art BUT on film. A bare midriff and ample cleavage is okay, however if anyone is kissed on the mouth in a movie then all hell breaks loose. Heaven forbid you see a bare breast with the forbidden nipple exposed... this only happens in the most rare of instances if it even makes it past the government censors or in assorted art-house endeavors.

Sex scenes have become "steamier" with quick cuts and arty cinematography. The same can be said of the supernatural elements for newer films. Cheap Halloween masks and gorilla suits have been replaced with bad computer graphics and paranormal activity. Rajkumar Kohli's **JAANI DUSHMAN: EK ANOKHI KAHANI**, the 2002 remake of his classic 1979 film **JANNI DUSHMAN**, is a perfect example of what was going to be the future of Indian horror films. Aped Hollywood-style editing, sex, and a sub-game quality computer animated monster destroyed what could have been a mildly intriguing film.

Another recent example is Pawan Kripalani's **RAGINI MMS** (2011) which is a crapfest of badly composed sexy scenes mashed-up with "found footage" of strange paranormal happenings. The film's voyeuristic meandering captures a couple's love making during one of their "dirty weekend" getaways at a haunted house. Not even the writhing sweaty forms of our attractive actors, Raj Kumar Yadav and Kainaz Motivala, can save this dreary production.

As luck would have it there are a few exceptions to the rule and these include Wilson Louis's non-musical straight-ahead *chudail* (witch-ghost) inspired **KAALO** (2010, reviewed in this issue), Jennifer Lynch's US-Indian co-production re-telling of the classic - and still very popular - Nagin cobra goddess film called **HISSS** (2010), and Vikram Bhatt's **RAAZ 3: the THIRD DIMENSION** (2012).

It may seem that horror hasn't gone away in India, nevertheless nothing can rival that boom of previous decades. The scene has changed along with other "A Certificate" films. More skin and even some lip-locking has been taking place in mainstream productions. What was once considered taboo is now increasingly becoming the norm. That's not a bad thing, but the more flesh you have in the mainstream, the less there is to fuel those films outside of the system. Some would consider the demise of "Grade C" films to be a blessing in disguise. I only find that possibility to be sad.

## *DISCLAIMER...*

*If this is the first time you've read anything concerning Indian horror films I'll let you in a little secret. All of this has been new for me as well. In fact, for every issue to follow I'll be reviewing films that I have never seen; digging up as much obscure information and details that I can. As stated part one of this column I am not an expert when it comes to these films, so, please, if I make a mistake call me out.*

*Special thanks to Chaitanya Reddy and Cara Romano for making this article possible.*

# Words of Wisdom: Names of the Beasts

Most of the fun in writing this type of article is in the hunt for source material. In the case of Indian horror films I didn't have a lot to go on. The always enticing cover art of the VCDs were always a draw. Over time I was able to decipher many of the romanized Hindu titles through key words. And as these are romanized words the exact spelling isn't always key. NAGIN could also be NAAGIN, and SHAITAN has numerous variants. But you'll get the idea. My title checker for this article, Chaitanya Reddy was also a great help. So, for any of you who want to take a chance at a film just by its title, be my guest. All you need is a lot of patience and look for the following words somewhere in the film's description. I can't guarantee the find of the lifetime, but you will always have something spooky in the mix:

**RAAT** - **Night** or **Dark**. Used in a lot of mysteries as well as horror film titles.

**AATMA** - **spirit** or **ghost**. Oh yea!

**BHOOT** - **evil spirit**, sometime found in conjunction with "aatma", "pyaasi" or "shaitan".

**PYAASI** - **thirsty**, contextual meaning in these horror movie would be thirst for blood mostly or revenge.

**NAGIN** - **snake woman**, popular demon or goddess in many films.

**MAHAL** - **building/monument/mansion**; typically associated with ghosts or some kind of haunting.

**LAASH** - **body** or **corpse**. Usually a good sign that you just have come across a mystery film in the very least.

**SHAITAN** - **demonic spirit**. Associated with the evil form of Djinn or elemental. Usually very devil-like. There are slight spelling variations, but they all mean the same thing.

**CHUDAIL** - **witch**; any film with this in the title is almost 100% horror oriented.

**KHOONI** - **bloody**, great adjective in any title.

**MAUT** - **death**. Plain and simple. Not a word you would usually associate with comedies.

**TANTRIK** - or **trantric** is the guy who makes people believe that he can drive away evil spirits. Not always a bad thing, and if this word is in the film's title, then you can be guaranteed some witchy fun.

**CHEEKH** - **shriek/scream**, self explanatory.

**MAUT** - **death**. Plain and simple.

# THE BOOKSHELF

***Transliterated from the back of the book:***

"Hand-painted film posters from Ghana are highly prized collectors items. They are cover all genre of film: prehistoric stories, war, karate sci fi, fantasy, gore, heroic fantasy... and the prices for them are rising. There have even been exhibited in art galleries all over the world.

The surreal look of these paintings has the public talking about the form of expression called "automatic painting" *[or possibly "outsider art" as it is popularly known as in the USA - editor]*. Ghana is a charming country of West Africa between The Ivory Coast and Togo. At the beginning of the 80s cinema theaters in Ghana were equipped with 35mm projectors, the remains of the auspicious British Empire. The projectors have long since wore out and broke down. With the beginning of video, some companies wanted to show movies in the more remote places of the country. They trained "pilot technicians" ready for the adventure. Sometimes with only a TV set and a VCR these knights of culture traveled the roads, stopping at video retailer shops, or setting up under a tent or outside venues. These people asked the local artists to create original poster art, not too similar to the actual film, but an idealized poster to impressed the local population.

Rustic Ghanese symbolism dominated the visuals. The artist prefer the "choc" to the "chic"; phantasm to reality, sharing innocently his fears, his credulity, and even his ancestral rites, which explains the proliferation of skulls, blood explosions, refined tortures, over-dimensioned guns, bulging muscles, beheadings, skeletons on the loose, cut members, lots of reptiles, various malformations, a monstrous bestiary finely painted with loud, gaudy colors.

The mood, sweetly fun, takes unexpected proportions when the author undertakes a perilous pictorial parallel between this, the typical naive Ghanian art, and the symbolism of the intellectual professionalism of the art world."

A beautifully presented large-size book on the weird, wacky and utterly wonderful world of hand-painted movie posters from Ghanna, Africa. Most of the art in this book was created for Western movies (and some local films) that were available to rent in video shop or watch in video parlors. Although entirely in French, this text-heavy 150 page tome is lavishly illustrated with color reproductions of this astounding artwork on heavy glossy stock. Well worth the cost of 22 euros + 10 euros S&H to the USA; contact and PayPal payment through **flambot@metalunaproductions.com**. From J.P. PUTTERS, the original publisher of the French cinema magazine "Mad Movies" that has been publishing since 1972. Special thanks to Marcel Burel for assistance and help in this review.

**AMBER SKOWRONSKI** is a special effects artist and illustrator living in Los Angeles. She is available for commissions and you can find her portfolio at *amberskowronski.brushd.com*

# EXPLOITATION RETROSPECT # 51
After a 13 year hiatus the print version of EXPLOITATION RETROSPECT is back! The journal of junk culture and fringe media celebrates its long-overdue 51st issue with articles on Ozploitation, the Gothic Horrors of Barbara Steele, NOSFERATU IN VENICE, the porn and wrestling connection and Bruno Mattei's THE JAIL. Plus a heaping helping of zine, comic and trash sinema reviews for your reading pleasure. Visit dantenet.com to order or send $5 cash to PO Box 5531, Lutherville, MD 21094-5531. (Available 10/1/12)

# THE HUNGOVER GOURMET:
The Journal of Food, Drink, Travel and Fun debuted in 1995 and ran until its final (?) issue in 2009. Topics include everything from cheesesteaks and the final days of Oliver Reed to crabcake eating competitions and celebrating places that are gone. Contributors include Dan Taylor, Tom Crites, Louis Fowler and legendary SLEAZOID EXPRESS publisher Bill Landis. Visit hungovergourmet.com for complete ordering details."

# A DEMOCRAZY OF BRAINDRAINED LOONS:
# THE FILMS OF MICHAEL LEGGE
BY DOUGLAS WALTZ
https://tsw.createspace.com/title/3814218
List Price: $9.99 , 74 pages
Douglas Waltz examines the films of micro budget film maker Michael Legge and his decision to go with comedy in the face of mountains of micro budget horror films clogging the countryside.

# SASQUATCH VS EL CHUPACABRA/
# THE PENULTIMATE MACHINATIONS OF FU MANCHU
BY DOUGLAS WALTZ
https://tsw.createspace.com/title/3946692
List Price: $6.99 , 34 pages
In the first 3/4 Time Publication you get two stories for the price of one. First, Beasts of Legend, Sasquatch and El Chupacabra are brought together in a fight to the finish. And then pulp fiction returns as super hero The Scythe must use all of his skills versus the legendary madman, Fu Manchu. And how does Waldemar Daninsky fit into this?

# GIMP: THE RAPENING VOLUME UNO
Join legendary (not really) cult cinema critic and published (barely) author Brian Harris has he introduces readers to exclusive online reviews spanning almost a decade of writing. From the sublime sleaze of European exploitation to the gag-inducing underground gore of Asia, Mr. Harris paints a picture of unhinged cinema the likes of which only the most depraved genre fans are capable of enjoying. GIMP: THE RAPENING VOLUME UNO collects together the first five previously published GIMP film guides into one massive tome of useless opinions. Never has a book more deserved to be purchased, read and burned than GIMP: THE RAPENING VOLUME UNO.

# GIMP: THE RAPENING VOLUME DEUX
Back again with a book sequel nobody in their right mind would demand, Brian Harris returns with yet more cinema reviews, this time collecting together unpublished material. Originally meant to be released as the next five installments in the original GIMP film guide series, GIMP: THE RAPENING VOLUME DEUX offers up even more senselessly offensive and unbelievably unnecessary opinions on films only the dregs of society could enjoy. Now with more potty language and references to midgets, GIMP: THE RAPENING VOLUME DEUX takes the success of the first book and squeezes consumers for just a bit more support and money. Purchase a copy now!

# GIMP: THE RAPENING VOLUME TRE
Seriously, nobody asked for this. No publishing company forced him to complete this. GIMP: THE RAPENING VOLUME TRE is a money grab, plain and simple. Take it. Take it all. You're going to love it, Brian Harris swears he'll only stick the tip in. Once you think it's not all that bad, he'll plunge it in, leaving you physically tattered and emotionally betrayed. It doesn't get better than this, forget WATCHING exploitation, now you've got the chance to BE exploited! COMING SOON!

The GIMP book series can be purchased through
AMAZON.COM and BARNESANDNOBLE.COM!

# PREMONITIONS: Causes For Alarm
Science fiction, horror stories, and genre poetry. At least a dozen cutting-edge speculative tales in every issue! Fiction by Matt Bright, Andrew Darlington, Waldo Gemio, Peter Hagelslag, David Howard, Patrick Hudson, William Jackson, Sue Lange, David McGillveray, Matthew Pendleton, Steven Pirie, Cyril Simsa, Jim Steel, Julie Travis, andFred Walker. Poetry from Cardinal Cox, J.C. Hartley, John Hayes, Steve Sneyd, and J.P.V. Stewart
Cover artists: Chris Moore, Caroline O'Neal
160 pages in A5 paperback • Order direct from the publisher: www.pigasuspress.co.uk

## FOR YOUR PRIVATE COLLECTION

It's happened! Kronos Productions has completely SOLD OUT of MONSTER! INTERNATIONAL # 1 & 2 and all issues of HIGHBALL MAGAZINE. But you can still get limited copies of #3 and 4 – and the remaining back issues are going fast! Better get yours now - while the short supply lasts!

#3 - Jose Mojica Marins, Possession films. more!

Our MONSTER! #4/HIGHBALL #3 Special Double Issue! Full of Babes and Beasts! Man or Astroman? Flexi Disc! More!!

**MONSTER! BACK ISSUES**
TIMOTHY PAXTON, CRYPT KEEPER
26 WEST VINE STREET
OBERLIN 44074 OH USA

I enclosed $............for the following issues:

☐ #3 $5.00 PPD USA      ☐ #4 $5.00 PPD USA
  $8 PPD WorldWide        $8 PPD WorldWide

NAME.................................................
ADDRESS.............................................
CITY................................ZONE.........
STATE...............................................

U.S. ORDER BY PAYPAL : ORLOF@ OBERLIN.NET
OR U.S. POSTAL ORDERS
INTERNATIONAL ORDERS PAYAPL ONLY

## WENG'S CHOP SPECIAL ISSUE ZERO!

The zine that started all this madness! Digest-size, 56 pages, color cover, reviews, articles, interviews! If you liked Weng's Chop #1 you'll go bonkers over SPECIAL ISSUE ZERO! Available from amazon.com -or- we have a limited supply of our first printing for only $5 PPD USA & Canada or $8 PPD overseas. Paypal: orlof@oberlin.net. Offer good while supplies last!

### Steve Bissette

is forever peddling all manner of his own comics (S.R. BISSETTE'S TYRANT®, SPIDERBABY COMIX, etc.), anthologies (TABOO), books (THE VERMONT MONSTER GUIDE, TEEN ANGELS & NEW MUTANTS, etc.), *and* new horror/monster prints (TYRANT® IN SLUMBERLAND, ALPHABET OF ZOMBIES, etc.) via his online shop. Visit his store at srbissette.com/store/

*and happy horror hunting!*

Printed in Great Britain
by Amazon.co.uk, Ltd.,
Marston Gate.